Meal Prep

The Absolute Best Meal Prep Cookbo
Loss And Clean Eating – Quick, Easy,
Meal Prep Recipes

Table of Contents

Introduction

You may have come across the phrase, "If you fail to prepare, you are preparing to fail." This is a little harsh when you think about it, but it is very true. It is true especially when it comes to planning your meals. You and everybody around you are probably busy and it does get difficult to cook fresh meals everyday.

Irrespective of whether you are a mom or a student or even working full time, cooking everyday at home may seem like a mighty task. This is where meal prep comes into the picture. If you focus on clean eating and invest a few minutes per day in meal preps, you will be able to decrease your junk intake and also be able to consume healthy meals.

But what is meal prep? This could mean different things to people and it is essential that you identify the routine that works best for you. Meal prepping should ideally save you time when it comes to cooking a meal and also make it easier for you to make healthy food. You can choose to prepare all your meals – breakfast, lunch, dinner and snacks – or just one meal a day for as long as you need to. You could have to use the trial and error method to get to the routine that does not hamper with your lifestyle or your preferences. If you are in a hurry to get out of the door every morning, and the only breakfast you eat is a slice of bread that is store bought, then you can use meal prep and prepare breakfast every morning. The same goes for any other meal too – always prepare for them in advance.

In the course of this book, we are going to understand what meal prepping is and also help you switch to clean eating, so you get the best of home cooked meals prepared from the freshest ingredients available.

I want to thank you for choosing this book and I hope you enjoy the recipes mentioned here.

Chapter 1: Meal Prep 101

You may have come across the phrase, "If you fail to prepare, you are preparing to fail." This is a little harsh when you think about it, but this is very true. It is true especially when it comes to planning and preparing your meals. You and everybody around you are probably busy and it does get difficult to prepare meals. Irrespective of whether you are a mom or a student or even working full time, it gets very difficult to cook a full meal at home on a regular basis. This is where meal prep comes into the picture. You will be able to prepare healthy meals that will last you for a week. This reduces the consumption of fast food and other junk, thereby preventing the deterioration of your health.

What is meal prep? This could mean different things to people and it is essential that you identify the routine that works best for you. You can prepare all your meals in advance to save time over the week or for a few days. If you are a beginner, you may want to take it slow. But, if you are someone who has done this before, you can prepare every meal for a week and store it in the refrigerator or the deep freeze.

You can choose to prepare all your meals – breakfast, lunch, dinner and snacks – or just meals for a day for as long as you need to. You must use the trial and error method to get to the routine that does not hamper with your lifestyle or your preferences. If you are someone who is in a hurry to get out of the door every morning, and the only breakfast you eat is a slice of bread from the store nearby, you will find that meal prepping over the weekend is the best thing for you. The same goes for any other meal too – always prepare for them in advance. You will be able to improve on your eating methods and will also be able to add some nutrition into your meals.

How to Meal Prep?
There are two approaches of meal prepping that have gained popularity over the years. The first approach is to cook and store meals for months together. You can prepare meals that will last between one and six months. But, to make life easier, you can prepare all your meals for a week. When it comes to prepping your meals in advance, you will need to be able to store them in containers like glass or Tupperware to ensure that they do not spoil easily. You will need to remember that the food you prep will need to be heated and for this reason, it is always good to get the containers that are BPA free and will definitely not melt in an oven.

The second approach is where you will only need to create the base for the meal. Let us assume that you have planned to eat a salad on Monday for lunch. On Sunday, you can chop the vegetables and prepare the dressing that will be going on the salad. You will not have to plan elaborately when it comes to this approach. The first approach, however, requires immense planning and great organization skills.

If you choose to prepare meals for a week or for a month, you will have to ensure that you have organized the refrigerator. You could choose to color code the days of the week or the meals. What you must remember is that the containers should essentially be of the same size. Try to avoid playing Tetris in your refrigerator.

There are a few steps that you will need to follow when it comes to prepping meals in advance.

Plan

Before you start the whole process of meal prepping, you will need to plan. If you are a beginner, you have to make sure that you take baby steps to avoid being overwhelmed. You may find it difficult to prepare a week's worth of meals even if you are a great cook. The biggest tip one could offer you here is to make sure that you set a plan that is manageable. It is always good to stick to just a few days as opposed to a week. This is only to help you get into the groove of the process.

It is extremely important to have a plan. It is a waste of time and money to go to a grocery store and put things into the cart and come back home to find a bunch of stuff that will not help you with making a meal. For meal prepping to work, you will need to have a plan, which states the different foods you will be making for a few days. You can stick to three or four days and write down what food you will be consuming for breakfast, lunch, dinner and snacks. Once you have identified your foods, you will need to list the ingredients needed for each of those foods. It is always good to stick to recipes that you have already used in the beginning. You will avoid making food that you do not like to eat.

Another thing to remember is to choose recipes that can be prepared much in advance and do not spoil. If you like oats, you can choose to have oats for breakfast the next morning. That way you will be able to store the oats overnight in the refrigerator.

Prep

There are numerous ways to prep the foods that you have planned. This section has some ways that you can use. Make sure that you choose the best way for you.

Food that tastes amazing will never go to waste. If you are someone who loves tasting different kinds of food, you can try to incorporate recipes into your diet that taste brilliant but are also along the lines of clean eating. You can experiment with different types of flavors and spices, which will go well with your food. However, if you are trying this for the first time, try to keep the experimenting at bay for the first few days.

Always try to incorporate variety into your meals. Try to mix and match certain foods to make sure that your meals taste better and look better. This way you will be able to avoid getting bored of eating the same kinds of food every single day.

Time

It has been mentioned that if this is the first time that you are trying meal prep, you should only prepare for a few meals at a time. Try to stick to two or three days initially to avoid being overwhelmed. However, the amount of time that you dedicate to preparing your meals is completely dependent on you.

If you think you will need an entire day to prepare meals for the next few days, you can go ahead and plan for that. However, you can also choose to prepare meals every night so that you can wake up and relax the following morning. The time you will be spending on preparing your meals is always dependent on the meals you will be preparing.

For instance, if your snack only has nuts in them, you will only have to wake up the following morning and pack yourself a tiny box with mixed nuts in them. You will not have to stay up the entire night just to prepare a meal. However, if you have a meal that is very complex, you will need to plan in advance and also prep in advance. It is for this reason that it is necessary that you have the perfect plan.

You can choose the approach that suits you best. It is always good to have a clear picture in mind to ensure that you do not over – prepare or under – prepare.

Cooking

Meal prep exists to make your life easy during the week. But, this does not mean that you need to prepare your meals in advance and leave them in the refrigerator. For instance, let us assume that you are making a chicken breast roast for lunches following day. You can marinade the chicken breasts and leave them in the freezer till you need to use them. On the day that you need to use them to make your meal, you will simply need to defrost them. The same thing applies to any other kind of meat.

If you are someone who likes to cook the vegetables fresh, you will need to portion them out, chop them and store them in the refrigerator till they need to be used. If you have a meal that needs a lot of ingredients to be chopped or ground, you can do this in advance to ensure that you save the time that goes into grinding or chopping the ingredients. It is always good to cook the carbohydrates like brown rice, pasta and quinoa right before the meal since they do not take too long to cook.

13

If you keep these points in mind, you will be able to prepare meals that taste lovely and adhere to the clean eating lifestyle.

Why is it important to meal prep?

People have enough time to make a meal for themselves that are healthy. What they do not have is the patience to make a healthy meal. Meal prepping helps to save a lot of time over the week. You can prepare your meals over the weekend and will only need to fire up the oven or the electric cooker to heat your food. Cooking over the weekend or even the night before may seem like an arduous task. But, it is important to understand that meal prepping can help you achieve all your nutrition goals. You will be able to assess what you can eat, how much you should eat and also understand the essence of a balanced diet.

You have to ensure that you have a few staple foods that you can cook in batches for the week or use in different ways to make your meals different and healthy. This is an essential point to remember. If you have absolutely no time, you can always choose to have tinned fish, salads, fruits, raw vegetables and nuts. These literally take no time to prepare. You will just need to chop them or season them and throw them into a container and store in the refrigerator.

You will find that the time you take out to prepare your meals for a week will definitely be rewarded with. Let us take a look at how.

Better Nutrition

When you have every meal planned for a week or for a month, you will avoid going to the local café or to the food cart at work for food.

The meals that you prepare will be nutritious. You will be able to ensure that the food you eat has the right amount of carbohydrates, fats and proteins. These will help in keeping your body healthy. Since you will reduce the junk food that you will be consuming, you will find that your weight has started to reduce. When you meal prep, you have the power to decide the ingredients that you will be using and the portions for each meal, which will help in weight loss.

Better Metabolism and health

Hunger strikes us at the oddest of times. You could be in the middle of a meeting and your stomach could start to growl. This is where meal prepping comes to the rescue. You would have had the time over the weekend to prepare a snack that is so nutritious and nourishing that you will not be hungry anymore. You will be able to avoid the biscuits that were laid out in front of you at the meeting.

14

When you give your body meals during intervals, your metabolism will improve. If you do not give your body nutritious food when you are hungry, you will find that your body has kicked into its catabolic state where the lean body tissue will be used up to provide your body with the energy needed. Meal prepping will help you avoid this state since you will be able to up your metabolism by snacking on nutritious food at intervals.

Saves money and time

This is a major advantage that everyone will want to grab. You will be able to eat healthy meals and will also be able to save time and money! You can skip the $20 that you may spend on a salad with a dressing that is not healthy and save $140 dollars a week. You can spend a little bit of that money on groceries and still save enough.

You will not be spending too much time on preparing food every morning. Instead, you will just have to heat the food that you have prepared over the weekend. You can still finish all your chores in the morning and also consume a healthy meal.

Chapter 2: Practical Tips to Make Meal Prepping Easy

You have read about how meal prepping saves you from giving into fast food or any other alternative food that is not healthy. You will be able to consume healthy meals when you start prepping your meals for an entire week.

Through meal prep, you will be able to achieve all your fitness goals and will be able to use budget – friendly ways to feed yourself and your family. There are numerous companies that have begun to sell meal prepped food and the ingredients for meal prepping. But, that will get expensive and will probably have foods that you may not like. It is always good to do your own meal prepping. If you set aside a few hours on a Sunday to prepare meals for the week, you will be saving money and time in the long run.

Before you rush to the grocery store, there are a few tips that you will need to keep in mind to ensure that you make most out of what you have purchased at the supermarket. You could also choose to weigh the carbohydrates, fats and proteins that you will be purchasing to assess the nutrition value of your food.

Let us take a look at a few tips to help make meal prepping easy.

Containers

The importance of containers was mentioned earlier. You have to make sure that you have containers that can be placed in the microwave or the oven without the fear of them melting. It is best to choose containers that are BPA free.

You have to remember that containers are a very important aspect to consider if you have decided to prepare meals for a week.

Spices and Condiments

When someone says that you must eat healthy, the first thought that comes into anyone's mind is that the food needs to be bland. But, this is not the case. You can make any meal tasty and savory by adding the right combination of spices and condiments. You can change the spices on a regular basis to break the monotony. You can prepare the same meal or recipe just by mixing up the spices and condiments.

You can use herbs to make your food fresh and have wonderful smell and taste. If you are going to be using condiments, you can mix them up in different jars and use them while preparing the meals.

You can use sea salt, cumin, red pepper, chili powder and paprika to spice your meals without having to worry about your caloric intake. If you choose to cook meals on Sunday, you can season the vegetables and protein with the different dressings and leave them inside the refrigerator to marinade. This will enhance the flavor of the food. You can add sauces and other dressings to the food just before you cook them. Always choose the approach that suits you best.

Proteins

Proteins are essential to restore tissues and strengthen the muscles in your body. They also help you maintain your energy levels throughout the day. Every meal that you consume contains one protein, carbohydrate and a portion of vegetables, but every meal you make depends on your health goals.

A person who is a meat eater will be able to select a protein very easily. You could choose from ground turkey to a chicken breast or any fish without giving it a second thought. You have to remember that a portion of protein for a day should fit into your palm – you can only eat 6 – 8 ounces of protein a day. You will need to toss the protein in the spices or marinade them depending on the meal you will be making. Make sure that you use cooking spray while cooking the meat instead of oil.

If you are a vegetarian, you should choose plant – based proteins like kidney beans, black beans, tofu or edamame. Quinoa is a grain that can be used as a carbohydrate portion in a vegetarian meal; it also helps to sneak in a few more proteins into a meatless diet.

Carbohydrates

There are a few weight loss diets that limit the intake of carbohydrates; however, these are key nutrients that help to break down the protein. They also help your body absorb the protein, which would help in providing you with energy. A balanced diet must always have a 3:1 ratio of carbohydrates to protein unless your diet requires a different ratio.

When it comes to carbohydrates, it is always good to turn to complex carbohydrates and whole grains since they keep you full till it is time for your next meal. Quinoa, pasta, whole wheat, buckwheat and rice like brown, wild grain; jasmine and basmati are the best carbohydrate option for meal prep. You can consume these with vegetables –mixed or unseasoned.

Vegetables

Leafy greens like kale, spinach and romaine are the healthiest options when it comes to choosing vegetables. If you do not want to make the usual salads using cucumbers, tomatoes, carrots and other veggies, you can sauté broccoli, asparagus and mushrooms to add flavor to your salads. Instead of buying spaghetti or pasta noodles, you can use zucchini or cucumber to make noodles that can be incorporated into your meals. It is important to remember that vegetables must take up half the space in the container.

Snacks and Sides

It is important to consume snacks in between meals to keep hunger afar. If you have not consumed fruits for breakfast, lunch or dinner, they would be the perfect snack for you.

Nuts are a great choice of snack since they can be mixed into just about anything – Greek yogurt or even a blend of fruits. You can simply zip the snack in a plastic bag or a container and take it with you.

You can have celery sticks, rice cakes or even peanut butter to keep your metabolism up. Protein bars are also a good option, but it is important that you find the right brand. There are a lot of bars that have entered the market claiming they are healthy. You may need to verify whether these bars are actually healthy before you begin consuming them.

Chapter 3: Common Mistakes

When it comes to meal prepping, there are a few mistakes that most beginners and experienced people make. This chapter will help you identify the mistakes that you should try to avoid to make your life easier.

Preparing too much Food

You do not always have to play it safe when it comes to meal prep. When you prepare too much food, you will be left with more than what you can eat. If you have not identified it, you may end up consuming more food than necessary. All you need to do is measure the amount of food you will need and cook according to that number.

If you make too much and do not finish it all, you will be wasting a lot of food and that is a waste of money and your time. It is always good to understand how much food you can eat till you have to throw it out. Food usually lasts only for five – seven days in the refrigerator after which you will need to freeze it. The only other option is to throw the leftovers out.

Preparing too little Food

If you are trying to stick to your portions, there could be a possibility that you have made less food. It can get very annoying if you have run out of food by Wednesday. The other option would be to consume very small meals that will not satiate your hunger. You may want to compensate that hunger by eating too many snacks or by consuming an extremely large meal later, or sometimes maybe both.

When you start meal prepping, you may not be able to find the right solution to avoid under – preparing. When you just start out, you will not be able to assess the right amount of food you will need. It is always good to take note of how you feel after a meal to help you understand if you need to increase or decrease your portions. This way you will be able to get the hang of cooking the correct amount of food after a few weeks.

Using Store Bought Sauces

Every sauce that you buy in the supermarket contains more calories and sugar as opposed to ones that you make at home. You can try to make your own sauces at home to avoid those extra calories in store bought sauces. If you do not want to make sauces, you will need to choose spices and other condiments to go with your meals. You can make simple dressings using olive oil and herbs that will enhance the flavor of your meals.

Cooking Food you do not Like

This happens to every single person. You probably make a lot of food that is healthy for you and that you will eat it and like it. But, that is not the case. When you start digging into the meal, you will remember things like, 'I do not like broccoli' or how you do not like the chicken without a marinade or barbecue sauce.

This is a waste of all your efforts. Instead of going for food that you do not like eating, prepare the food that you do like to eat but try to keep it healthy. Instead of butter, you could use olive oil. Try to find healthier alternatives for some ingredients. Then you will be able to eat every meal you consume.

If you keep these points in mind, you will be able to make meal prep a success for you.

Chapter 4: Frequently Asked Questions

If you are new to meal prepping, you could have questions on getting started. Let us take a look at a few questions that are frequently asked.

Should meals be frozen or refrigerated?

If you are not going to be consuming a meal within three days, it is best to freeze it. When you freeze your meals, they will be fresh for a longer period of time. The night before you will need to consume the meal, you can move it to the refrigerator to thaw and then heat the meal in the microwave or oven.

How long can food be stored in the freezer?

There are certain foods that can be stored longer in the freezer while there are others that should not be frozen. The FDA has a chart that gives you the correct indication. It is best to follow this to avoid spoiling the meals you have prepared.

It would be best to not freeze leafy vegetables and other foods with higher water content since they become soggy. The same goes for pasta. However, you can store meat and veggies in the freezer without too much worry.

What size must the containers be?

When you have decided on your food portions, you will be able to assess the size of the containers you will need to use. It is best to keep the same portions for every meal over the week.

How much food should you prepare?

This depends on your caloric needs. On an average, a man would need 2500 calories a day to maintain his health while a woman would need 2000 calories. However, this requirement may change depending on the age and other factors.

Should the same food be consumed throughout the week?

You may be preparing food for five or seven days, but this does not mean that you consume the same food on all days. But, there is no harm in doing this since you will love the food that you prepare. However, there are ways to add variety to your meals.

- Skip a meal or two from your meal prep and eat something else. You can make food that you love but ensure that the food that you are eating satisfies your fitness and health goals.

- Add different vegetables and sauces to your meals. This will give them a different taste and flavor.

- There are a few people who prefer to stick to two types of meals during the week. You can choose to make different types of meals for the entire week. This will increase your time in the kitchen on Sunday.

Chapter 5: Three Week Meal Plan

Week 1

Day 1:
Breakfast - Rainbow Chard Ginger Fruit Smoothie
Lunch - Curried Chicken over Spinach
Snack - Kale Chips
Dinner - Sausage and Cauliflower Bake
Dessert - Chocolate Pudding

Day 2
Breakfast - Simple Oats
Lunch - Chicken Parmesan
Snack - Crispy Edamame Popcorn
Dinner - Pulled Pork Poblano
Dessert - Black Forest Banana Split

Day 3
Breakfast - Super Foods Smoothie
Lunch - Chicken Taco Pizza
Snack - Chili -Lime Spiced Pumpkin Seeds
Dinner Coconut Red Pork Curry
Dessert - Coconut and Chia seed Pudding

Day 4
Breakfast - Whole Wheat Buttermilk Pancakes
Lunch - Chicken Paprika
Snack - Veggie Lettuce Wraps
Dinner Shepherd's Pie
Dessert - Strawberry/ Blueberry Ice cream

Day 5
Breakfast - Peach N Oats Smoothie
Lunch - Coconut Shrimp and Avocadoes
Snack - Spinach Hummus Pinwheel Wraps
Dinner - Zucchini Pasta Bolognese
Dessert - Puffed Quinoa Peanut Butter Balls

Day 6
Breakfast – Slimmin Citrus Smoothie
Lunch - Beef Taco Stuffed Avocadoes
Snack - Egg and Avocado Salad
Dinner - Curried Chicken over Spinach
Dessert - Carrot Cake Energy Bites

Day 7
Breakfast - Spinach Omelet Roll-Up
Lunch - Seared Salmon in Green Peppercorn Sauce
Snack - Chicken Fingers
Dinner Beef Taco Stuffed Avocadoes
Dessert - No Bake Cookies

Week 2

Day 1
Breakfast - Avocado Vanilla Smoothie
Lunch - Grilled Teriyaki Pork Lettuce Wraps
Snack - Fish Sticks
Dinner - Rosemary Lamb Chops
Dessert - Orange Berry Parfait

Day 2
Breakfast - Egg White and Avocado Bake
Lunch - Shrimp and Bacon skillet
Snack - Guacamole Devilled Eggs
Dinner - Beef and Broccoli Stir Fry
Dessert - Strawberry Mousse

Day 3
Breakfast - Flat - Belly Smoothie
Lunch - Easy Tuna Sliders
Snack - Pita Pizza
Dinner Lamb Roast with Veggies
Dessert - Pumpkin Pie Yogurt Parfait

Day 4
Breakfast - Savory Breakfast Casserole
Lunch - Shrimp and Bacon skillet

Snack - Chilled Avocado Soup
Dinner - Homemade Burgers
Dessert - Honey-Broiled Nectarines

Day 5
Breakfast - High Energy Breakfast Smoothie
Lunch - Sausage and Cauliflower Bake
Snack - Avocado Cashew Salad
Dinner - Chicken Parmesan
Dessert - Nutty Blueberry Protein Balls

Day 6
Breakfast - Breakfast Bagel
Lunch - Coconut Red Pork Curry
Snack - Egg and Avocado Salad
Dinner Grilled Teriyaki Pork Lettuce Wraps
Dessert - Carrot Cake Energy Bites

Day 7
Breakfast - Tomato Frittata
Lunch - Pulled Pork Poblano
Snack - Chicken and Avocado Caesar Salad
Dinner Shrimp and Bacon skillet
Dessert - No Bake Cookies

Week 3

Day 1
Breakfast - Baked Denver Omelet
Lunch - Beef and Broccoli Stir Fry
Snack - Strawberry Cantaloupe Soup
Dinner Easy Tuna Sliders
Dessert - Nutty Blueberry Protein Balls

Day 2
Breakfast - Blueberry Tofu Protein Smoothie
Lunch - Beef Taco Stuffed Avocadoes
Snack - Potato Rounds with Fresh Lemon
Dinner - Seared Salmon in Green Peppercorn Sauce
Dessert - Honey-Broiled Nectarines

Day 3

Breakfast - Chocolate Raspberry Smoothie
Lunch - Shepherd's Pie
Snack - Simply Tasty Black Beans
Dinner - Coconut Shrimp and Avocadoes
Dessert - Puffed Quinoa Peanut Butter Balls

Day 4

Breakfast - Pizza Egg Muffins
Lunch - Homemade Burgers
Snack - Quinoa Salad with Asparagus, Dates, and Orange
Dinner - Chicken Paprika
Dessert - Pumpkin Pie Yogurt Parfait

Day 5

Breakfast - Fat burning Green Tea Smoothie
Lunch - Lamb Roast with Veggies
Snack - Halibut Salad
Dinner - Chicken Taco Pizza
Dessert - Coconut and Chia seed Pudding

Day 6

Breakfast - Breakfast Tacos
Lunch - Zucchini Pasta Bolognese
Snack - Seafood Gazpacho
Dinner - Chicken Parmesan
Dessert - Black Forest Banana Split

Day 7

Breakfast - Coconut Water Energy Smoothie
Lunch - Rosemary Lamb Chops
Snack - Raw Asian Broccoli Salad
Dinner - Curried Chicken over Spinach
Dessert - Chocolate Pudding

Chapter 6: Smoothie Recipes

Rainbow Chard Ginger Fruit Smoothie

Serves: 4

Ingredients:
- 12 ounces rainbow chard
- 2 cups frozen mango
- 2 inch pieces ginger, peeled, sliced
- 2 apples, cored, chopped
- 2 tablespoons chia seeds
- 1 ½ cups water
- Ice cubes as desired

Method:
1. Place all the ingredients in a blender and blend until smooth. Add more water if you desire a smoothie of thinner consistency. The smoothie will become thicker because of chia seeds.
2. Pour into tall glasses. Chill in the refrigerator in an airtight container.
3. Consume within 48 hours.

Super Foods Smoothie

Serves: 6

Ingredients:
- 2 small bananas, peeled, sliced, frozen
- 2 cups baby spinach
- 2 cups frozen berries of your choice
- 1 inch fresh ginger, peeled, sliced
- 2 cups green tea
- 1 cup kefir or low fat plain Greek yogurt
- 1 cup pomegranate juice

Instructions:
1. Prepare green tea and chill in the refrigerator.
2. Add all the ingredients into a blender and blend until smooth. Pour into tall glasses.
4. Chill in the refrigerator in an airtight container.
5. Consume within 48 hours.

Peach N Oats Smoothie

Serves: 6

Ingredients:
- 3 cups peeled, pitted, chopped peaches, frozen
- 1 cup almond milk
- 1 cup coconut milk
- 1 cup peach yogurt
- 1 cup oats
- 2 overripe bananas, peeled, chopped, frozen

Method:
1. Add all the ingredients into the blender and blend until smooth. Add more almond milk or coconut milk to dilute the smoothie if you desire a smoothie of thinner consistency. The smoothie will become thicker because of oats.
2. Pour into tall glasses. Chill in the refrigerator in an airtight container..
3. Consume within 48 hours.

Avocado Vanilla Smoothie

Serves: 4

Ingredients:
- 2 ripe avocadoes, peeled, pitted, chopped
- 2 cups pear nectar, unsweetened or more if required
- 1 teaspoon vanilla extract

Method:
1. Add all the ingredients to a blender and blend until smooth.
2. Chill in the refrigerator in an airtight container.
3. Consume within 48 hours.

Flat - Belly Smoothie

Serves: 4

Ingredients:
- 1 cup frozen blueberries
- 1 cup frozen pineapple, chopped
- 2 cups kale, hard stems and ribs removed, torn
- 6 ounces vanilla flavored, nonfat Greek yogurt
- 1 ½ cups water

Method:
1. Add all the ingredients into a blender and blend until smooth. Add more water to dilute the smoothie if you desire a smoothie of thinner consistency.
2. Chill in the refrigerator in an airtight container.
3. Consume within 48 hours.

Cantaloupe Smoothie

Serves: 2

Ingredients:

- 1 ½ cups cantaloupe pieces
- ¾ cup strawberries, chopped
- 6 romaine lettuce leaves

Method:

1. Add all the ingredients to the blender and blend until smooth. Add more water to dilute the smoothie if you desire a smoothie of thinner consistency.
2. Chill in the refrigerator in an airtight container.
3. Consume within 48 hours.

High Energy Breakfast Smoothie

Serves: 4

Ingredients:
- 1 large banana, chopped
- 1 cup strawberries, chopped
- 5 tablespoons almond butter
- 4 tablespoons ground flaxseeds
- 3 cups low fat milk or any other milk of your choice
- 3 tablespoons blackstrap molasses

Method:
1. Add all the ingredients into a blender and blend until smooth. Add more milk if you desire a smoothie of thinner consistency. The smoothie will become thicker because of flaxseeds.
2. Chill in the refrigerator in an airtight container.
3. Consume within 48 hours.

Antioxidant Smoothie

Serves: 2

Ingredients:
- 2 cups mixed berries
- 1 tablespoon chia seeds + extra for garnishing
- 1 cup pomegranate juice, unsweetened
- 1 cup water

Method:
1. Add all the ingredients to the blender and blend until smooth. Add more juice or water to dilute the smoothie if you desire a smoothie of thinner consistency. The smoothie will become thicker because of chia seeds
2. Chill in the refrigerator in an airtight container.
3. Sprinkle chia seeds on top just before serving.
4. Consume within 48 hours.

Blueberry Tofu Protein Smoothie

Serves: 4

Ingredients:
- 1 cup blueberries
- 2 tablespoons honey or to taste
- 1 large ripe banana, peeled, sliced
- 8 ounces soft silken tofu
- 2 cups soy milk or more according to the consistency you desire

Method:
1. Add all the ingredients into the blender and blend until smooth. Add more soymilk to dilute the smoothie if you desire a smoothie of thinner consistency.
2. Chill in the refrigerator in an airtight container.
3. Consume within 48 hours.

Coconut Water Energy Smoothie

Serves: 6

Ingredients:
- 2 cups pineapple, chopped
- 2 cups watermelon, deseeded, chopped
- 2 cups spinach, rinsed, torn
- 1 cup blueberries
- 3 cups coconut water or more if required
- 1 green apple, cored, chopped

Method:
1. Add all the ingredients to the blender and blend until smooth. Add more coconut water to dilute the smoothie if you desire a smoothie of thinner consistency.
2. Chill in the refrigerator in an airtight container..
3. Consume within 48 hours. (If you are using fresh pineapple, the smoothie tends to get slightly bitter with time)

Chocolate Raspberry Smoothie

Serves: 3

Ingredients:
- ½ cup chocolate chips
- 1 cup soy milk
- 2 cups fresh raspberries
- 12 ounces vanilla flavored yogurt

Method:
1. Add all the ingredients to the blender and blend until smooth. Add more soymilk to dilute the smoothie if you desire a smoothie of thinner consistency.
2. Chill in the refrigerator in an airtight container.
3. Consume within 48 hours.

Slimming Citrus Smoothie

Serves: 4

Ingredients:
- ½ grapefruit, peeled, separated into segments, deseeded, peel the segments
- 2 oranges, peeled, separated into segments, deseeded
- 5-6 strawberries
- 1 cup raspberries
- 1 cup spinach
- 2 tablespoons chia seeds
- 1 cup water

Method:
1. Add all the ingredients to the blender and blend until smooth. Add more water to dilute the smoothie if you desire a smoothie of thinner consistency. The smoothie becomes thicker because of chia seeds.
2. Chill in the refrigerator in an airtight container.
3. Consume within 48 hours.

Fat burning Green Tea Smoothie

Serves: 3

Ingredients:
- 1 cup broccoli florets
- ½ cup cauliflower florets
- 1 cup pineapple pieces
- 1 ½ cups caffeinated green tea or more according to the consistency you desire

Method:
1. Add all the ingredients into a blender and blend until smooth. Add more water to dilute the smoothie if you desire a smoothie of thinner consistency.
2. Chill in the refrigerator in an airtight container.
3. Consume within 48 hours. (If you are using fresh pineapple, the smoothie tends to get slightly with time.)

Chapter 7: Breakfast Recipes

Simple Oats

Serves: 5-6
Cook time: 10 minutes

Ingredients:
- 1 ½ cups rolled oats
- 1 cup water
- 4 tablespoons chia seeds
- 2 cups almond milk or any other milk of your choice
- 4 tablespoons coconut oil
- 1 cup mixed nuts of your choice, chopped
- 4 teaspoons ground cinnamon
- 4 tablespoons coconut yogurt or low fat plain yogurt
- Berries to serve (optional)

Method:
1. Add all the ingredients into a large bowl and mix well.
2. Transfer into mason jars. Fasten with lid.
3. Refrigerate until use.
4. It can last for up to 3 days.

Whole Wheat Buttermilk Pancakes

Serves: 4
Cook time: 15 minutes

Ingredients:

- 2 cups whole wheat flour
- 4 tablespoons brown sugar
- ¼ teaspoon cooking soda
- 2 cups buttermilk
- 1 teaspoon baking powder
- ¼ teaspoon salt
- Cooking spray
- Honey to serve
- Berries to serve
- Cooking spray

Method:

1. Mix together all the dry ingredients in a large bowl. Transfer into an airtight container until use.
2. To use: Pour buttermilk and whisk well until it is free from lumps. Set aside for 10-15 minutes.
3. Place a nonstick skillet over medium heat. Spray with cooking spray. Pour about a ladle of batter. (Or pour according to the size of pancakes you desire). Swirl the pan so that it spreads a little.
4. Bubbles will start appearing on the top of the pancake. Cook until the underside is golden brown (or the color you desire). Flip sides and cook the other side too. Remove carefully and keep warm.
5. Repeat steps 2 and 3 with the remaining batter.
6. Top with honey and berries.
7. Refrigerate until use. It can last for up to 3 days.
8. To serve: Microwave for 2 minutes and serve.

Spinach Omelet Roll-Up

Serves: 2
Cook time: 15 minutes

Ingredients:
- 2 eggs, beaten
- 2 teaspoons olive oil or canola oil
- 2 teaspoons olive tapenade
- 1/8 teaspoon red pepper flakes
- 2 tablespoons goat cheese, crumbled
- Salt to taste
- 2 cups baby spinach, torn

Method:
1. Place a skillet over medium heat. Add a teaspoon of oil. When the oil is heated, add half the beaten egg and swirl the skillet. Cook until the underside is done. Flip sides and cook the other side for a minute. Remove on to a plate.
2. Repeat the above step with the remaining egg.
3. Place the skillet back on heat and add spinach. Cook until the spinach wilts. Remove from heat. Cool the omelet.
4. Place the omelet on your work area. Spread 1-teaspoon tapenade on each of the cooked eggs.
5. Sprinkle half the goat's cheese and half the spinach on each. Sprinkle chili flakes and salt.
6. Roll up and place each in an airtight container. Pack some salsa or a dip of your choice along side. Cover with a lid.
7. Refrigerate until use. It can last for up to 3 days.
8. To serve: Microwave for about a minute and serve.

Savory Breakfast Casserole

Serves: 4
Cook time: 30 minutes

Ingredients:
- 6 eggs, whisked
- 1 small sweet potato, shredded
- ½ pound chorizo
- 1 tablespoon Sriracha sauce
- 1 small yellow onion, diced
- ½ teaspoon onion powder
- ½ teaspoon garlic powder
- ½ teaspoon pepper powder
- ½ teaspoon salt

Method:
1. Place a skillet over medium heat. Add chorizo and cook until it crumbles. Remove from heat and set aside.
2. Add chorizo, and rest of the ingredients to the bowl of whisked eggs. Whisk well.
3. Pour into a greased freezer-proof baking dish. Cover with foil and place in the freezer until use.
4. Bake in a preheated oven at 300° F for 30 minutes. Uncover and bake for 10 minutes or until set. Let it remain in the oven for 10 minutes before serving.
5. Chop into wedges.
6. Refrigerate until use. It can last for up to 3 days.
7. To serve: Microwave for 3 minutes and serve.

Egg White and Avocado Bake

Serves: 4
Cook time: 15 minutes

Ingredients:
- 10 egg whites
- 1 tablespoons butter, unsalted
- 2 ripe Hass avocadoes, peeled, pitted, sliced
- Salt to taste
- Pepper powder to taste

Method:
1. Whisk egg whites with salt and pepper. Add half the avocado slices.
2. Grease a baking dish with butter. Pour the egg white mixture into it. Cover with foil and place in the refrigerator until use.
3. It can last for 2 days if refrigerated.
4. Bake in a preheated oven at 375° F for about 30 minutes or until set. Let it remain in the oven for 5-8 minutes.
5. Chop into wedges and add the remaining avocado slices.
6. Refrigerate until use. It can last for up to 3 days.
7. To serve: Microwave for 2 minutes and serve.

Breakfast Bagel

Serves: 2
Cook time: 10 minutes

Ingredients:
- 2 large eggs
- 1 whole wheat bagel, halved, toasted
- 4 slices tomatoes
- 4 slices avocado
- 4 ounce low fat cheese
- 2 teaspoons apple cider vinegar
- Salt to taste
- Pepper powder to taste

Method:
1. Pour water and vinegar to a large shallow pan and place over high heat. Bring to a boil.
2. Lower heat and add eggs and cook until done. Remove the eggs with a slotted spoon and place them in separate small microwave safe containers. Cover and refrigerate until use. It can last for 2 days.
3. To serve: Microwave the poached eggs for 10-15 seconds. Place 2 slices tomatoes and 2 slices avocado on each half of toasted bagel. Sprinkle cheese over it. Place an egg each over the cheese. Sprinkle salt and pepper and serve.

Tomato Frittata

Serves: 3
Cook time: 40 minutes

Ingredients:
- 5 large eggs
- 3 bacon slices, chopped into small chunks
- 1 medium sized onions, thinly sliced
- 2 ounce baby spinach leaves
- 1 ripe tomato, thinly sliced
- 1 ½ teaspoon homemade mustard
- Fresh basil leaves for garnishing
- ½ tablespoon olive oil
- Sea salt to taste
- Pepper powder to taste

Method:
1. Whisk the eggs well. Add salt and pepper.
2. Heat olive oil in an ovenproof skillet. When oil is heated, add onions and bacon and sauté until the onions are golden brown.
3. Add spinach and sauté until the spinach wilts.
4. Pour the egg mixture over the onion mixture. Cook for about a minute.
5. Sprinkle tomatoes on top of the egg layer. When the sides are cooked and the middle undercooked, remove from heat.
6. Place the skillet in a preheated oven.
7. Bake at 375° F for around 20-25 minutes.
8. Cut into wedges and store in an airtight container.
9. Refrigerate until use. It can last for a week if refrigerated.
10. To serve: Remove from the refrigerator. Place as many slices as required in a baking dish.
11. Bake at 375° F for around 10-15 minutes.

Ricotta and Yogurt Parfait

Serves: 2

Ingredients:
- ½ cup part skim, ricotta cheese
- 1 ½ cups non-fat vanilla Greek yogurt
- ½ cup raspberries of any other berries of your choice
- 1 teaspoon lemon zest, grated
- 2 teaspoons chia seeds
- 2 tablespoons almonds, slivered

Method:
1. Add yogurt, ricotta cheese and lemon zest into a bowl and stir.
2. Divide into 2 parfait glasses. Cover with foil. Chill in the refrigerator until use.
3. It can last for 3-4 days if refrigerated.
4. To serve: Sprinkle chia seeds, raspberries, and almonds on top and serve.

Green Egg Bake

Serves: 3-4
Cook time: 20 minutes

Ingredients:
- 6 large eggs
- 1 large white onion, thinly sliced
- 6 cups collard greens, chopped
- 6 cups spinach, chopped
- 8 white mushrooms, sliced
- 6 cloves garlic, peeled, minced, divided
- 1 ½ tablespoons olive oil
- 1 teaspoon red pepper flakes or to taste
- 1 teaspoon dried oregano
- 1 ½ teaspoons ground cumin
- Freshly ground black pepper to taste
- Salt to taste
- 3 tablespoons Greek yogurt
- 4 teaspoons 1% milk or light coconut milk
- 3 teaspoons red chili paste
- Cooking spray

Method:
1. Place a heavy bottomed pan over medium high heat. Add oil. When oil is heated, add onion and sauté until onions turn light brown.
2. Add salt, pepper, and collard greens and cook for a couple of minutes until it turns bright green.
3. Add half the garlic, cumin, oregano, red pepper and sauté for a few seconds until fragrant.
4. Add spinach and cook until spinach wilts.
5. Remove from heat.
6. Spray a large freezer safe baking dish with cooking spray. Remove spinach mixture from the pot with a slotted spoon and add to the dish.
7. Place mushrooms all over it. Make 6 cavities (big enough to fit an egg) in the spinach mixture. Crack an egg into each of the cavity. Sprinkle salt and pepper.
8. Cover with foil. Place in the freezer until use.
9. To use: Place the dish in a preheated oven and bake at 400° F for 10-12 minutes. Uncover and bake until eggs are set to the consistency you desire.
10. Let it remain in the oven for 5 minutes before serving.

Breakfast Tacos

Serves: 4
Cook time: 10 minutes

Ingredients:
- 8 large eggs, lightly beaten
- 1 large onion, chopped
- 2 tablespoons extra virgin olive oil
- 4 cloves garlic, minced
- 12 medium tomatillos, husked, rinsed, coarsely chopped
- Salt to taste
- Pepper powder to taste
- ½ cup feta cheese, crumbled
- 8 small corn or whole wheat tortillas or taco shells

Method:
1. Place a skillet over medium heat. Add oil. When the oil is heated, add tomatillos, onion, and garlic and cook until almost dry.
2. Add eggs, salt, and pepper. Stir and cook until the eggs are set.
3. Place the tortillas on your work area.
4. Divide the mixture among the tortillas or taco shells. Garnish with cheese.
5. Place the tortillas in individual containers. Pack alongside some dip of your choice.
6. To serve: Microwave for about 20 seconds and serve.

Baked Denver Omelet

Serves: 3
Cook time: 30 minutes

Ingredients:
- 4 large eggs
- 1 small onion, finely chopped
- ¼ cup green bell pepper, finely chopped
- ¼ cup red bell pepper, finely chopped
- 2 teaspoons olive oil
- ½ cup cooked ham, chopped
- 3 tablespoons milk
- ¼ cup low fat cheddar cheese, shredded
- A dash of hot sauce to serve
- Chopped chives to serve
- Avocado slices to serve (optional)
- Salt to taste
- Pepper powder to taste

Method:
1. Place a skillet over medium high heat. Add oil. When the oil is heated, add onion and bell peppers and sauté until the vegetables are soft. Remove from heat.
2. Place the ham pieces in a small, greased baking dish. Transfer the cooked vegetables over it.
3. Sprinkle cheese over the vegetables.
4. Whisk together eggs, salt, pepper, and milk in a bowl and pour over the cheese in the baking dish.
5. Bake in a preheated oven at 400° F until set. Slice into wedges.
6. Pack the wedges into 2-3 containers.
7. To serve: Microwave the wedges.
8. Sprinkle chives. Dot with hot sauce and serve with avocado slices if desired.

Pizza Egg Muffins

Serves: 6
Cook time: 35 minutes

Ingredients:
- ½ cup broccoli, chopped, cooked
- 4 large eggs
- 4 ounce sliced mushrooms
- 1 tablespoon coconut milk or skim milk
- 2 tablespoons black olives, sliced
- 1 teaspoon canola oil
- ½ tablespoon pizza seasoning
- ¼ teaspoon salt or to taste
- ¼ teaspoon pepper powder or to taste

Method:
1. Place a skillet over medium high heat. Add oil. When the oil is heated, add mushrooms and sauté until light brown. Remove from heat and add broccoli and olives and stir.
2. Place a little of this mixture into lined and greased muffin tray to fill about ¾ each.
3. Whisk together in a bowl, eggs, milk, pizza seasoning, salt and pepper. Pour this mixture into the muffin tray over the vegetables so as to fill up to 2/3 each.
4. Place the muffin tray in a preheated oven and bake at 350° F for 20 -25 minutes or until a toothpick when inserted in the center of the muffin comes out clean. Run a knife around the edges of the muffin cups. Invert on to a plate.
5. Pack the muffins in an airtight container. Refrigerate until use.
6. To serve: Microwave for 15 seconds and serve with a dip of your choice.

Pumpkin-Papaya Acai Bowl

Serves: 6

Ingredients:

For the acai bowl:
- 1 cup papaya
- 1 cup canned pumpkin
- 2 medium bananas, sliced
- 2 frozen acai smoothie pack, unsweetened
- 1 tablespoon ground cinnamon
- 1 tablespoon pumpkin pie spice
- 2 tablespoons maca powder
- 2 cups almond milk

To serve:
- 1 cup goji berries
- ½ cup cashews, chopped, toasted
- A few slices papaya
- A few slices banana
- ½ cup pomegranate seeds
- ½ cup granola

Method:
1. Add all the ingredients of the acai bowl into the blender and blend until smooth. Divide and pour into 6 serving bowls. Cover with foil. Chill until use.
2. It can last for 24 hours if refrigerated.
3. To serve: Add papaya, banana, and pomegranate seeds and stir.
4. Sprinkle goji berries, cashews and granola on top and serve.

Chapter 8: Salad Recipes

Rainbow Soba Salad

Serves: 2
Cook time: 10 minutes

Ingredients:
- 1 cup green cabbage, shredded
- 2 kale leaves, discard hard stems and ribs, finely sliced
- ½ cup red cabbage, shredded
- ¾ tablespoon low sodium tamari
- 1 tablespoon rice vinegar
- ½ tablespoon honey
- 2 tablespoons sesame seeds, toasted
- 4 ounces buckwheat soba noodles to serve

Method:
1. To make dressing: Add vinegar, tamari and honey to a bowl and whisk well. Refrigerate until use.
2. Add all the vegetables to a bowl. Refrigerate until use.
3. To serve: Cook noodles according to the instructions on the package.
4. To serve: Pour the dressing over the salad. Toss well.
5. Add noodles and toss well.
6. Sprinkle sesame seeds and serve.

Halibut Salad

Serves: 3
Cook time: 10 minutes

Ingredients:
- 1 pound mixed salad greens, rinsed, pat dried
- 12 ounces halibut steaks or fillets
- 8 cloves garlic, peeled, pressed
- 2/3 cup fresh lemon juice
- 2 cups vegetable broth
- 1/3 cup fresh sage, minced or 2 tablespoons dried sage
- Salt to taste
- Pepper powder to taste
- 6 tablespoons extra virgin olive oil (optional)

Method:
1. Brush halibut steaks with lemon juice. Sprinkle salt and pepper.
2. Pour broth in a skillet. Place the skillet over medium heat. Add halibut, cover and cook until done.
3. Meanwhile, divide and place the salad greens in a serving bowl.
4. Remove the halibut from the pan and place over the greens.
5. Discard the broth.
6. Place the pan back on heat. Add garlic, sage and lemon juice and heat for half a minute.
7. If you are using olive oil add it after removing it from heat. Pour over the salad. Sprinkle some salt and pepper. Cover with cling wrap and refrigerate until use.
8. It can last for up to 2 days.

Quinoa Salad with Asparagus, Dates, and Orange

Serves: 2-3
Cook time: 30 minutes

Ingredients:

For the salad
- ½ cup quinoa, uncooked
- ¼ cup white onion, finely chopped
- ½ cup orange segments, deseeded, chopped
- ¼ pound asparagus, sliced, steamed, cooled
- 1 cup water
- 2 tablespoons pecans, toasted
- 1 tablespoon red onion, minced
- 3 dates, pitted, chopped
- ¼ teaspoon kosher salt or to taste
- ½ jalapeño pepper, sliced
- ½ teaspoon olive oil

For the dressing:
- ½ tablespoon extra virgin olive oil
- 1 clove garlic, minced
- 1 tablespoon lemon juice
- 1/8 teaspoon freshly ground black pepper
- 1/8 teaspoon kosher salt
- A handful of mint leaves, chopped + a few sprigs to garnish

Method:
1. Add orange, asparagus, pecans, red onion, dates, jalapeño pepper and oil into a large bowl and toss well. Chill until use.
2. To serve: Place a nonstick skillet over medium high heat. Add oil. When the oil is heated, add onions and sauté until onions are translucent.
3. Add quinoa and sauté for 3-4 minutes. Add water and salt and bring to the boil.
4. Lower heat, cover and simmer until water is dried up. Remove from heat and set aside covered for 15 minutes. Uncover, and fluff with a fork. Transfer into the bow of salad.
5. To make dressing: Add all the ingredients to a small bowl and whisk well. Alternately, add all the ingredients into a small glass jar. Cover tightly with a lid and shake vigorously until well combined.

6. Pour dressing over salad and toss again.
7. Garnish with mint sprigs and serve.

Caper and Lemon Salad

Serves: 6
Cook time: 10 minutes

Ingredients:
- 3 pounds salmon fillet
- Salt to taste
- Pepper to taste
- Juice of a lemon or to taste
- 1 teaspoon lemon zest, grated
- 1/3 cup canned capers, drained, rinsed
- 3 stalks celery, chopped
- 3 teaspoon fresh dill, chopped
- 3 tablespoons extra virgin olive oil

Method:
1. Place salmon in a baking dish. Season the salmon with salt and pepper. Bake in a preheated oven at 350° F for 10 minutes or until the salmon is flaky.
2. Transfer the salmon into a serving bowl. Add lemon juice, lemon zest, capers, celery, dill and olive oil and toss.
3. Place in the refrigerator until use. It can last for up to 2 days.

Raw Asian Broccoli Salad

Serves: 3-4

Ingredients:

For the salad:
- 2 large carrots, grated
- 1 large head broccoli, grated
- 2 large cucumbers, grated

For the dressing:
- 2 tablespoons soy sauce or coconut aminos
- 2 tablespoons almond butter
- 2 tablespoons honey or to taste
- 2 tablespoons white vinegar
- 1 tablespoon water
- 2 tablespoons sesame seeds

Method:
1. Add all the salad ingredients into a large bowl. Toss well. Chill until use. It can last for 24 hours if refrigerated.
2. To serve: Add all the dressing ingredients except water into a small bowl and whisk until well combined. Cover and set aside for 15 minutes. The dressing would have thickened. Add water and whisk again. Add more water if you find the dressing too thick.
3. Pour dressing over the salad. Toss well and serve.

Egg and Avocado Salad

Serves: 3
Cook time: 10 minutes

Ingredients:
- 2 avocados, peeled, pitted, mashed
- 6 hard boiled eggs, peeled, chopped
- 2 tablespoons sweet pickle relish
- 2 tablespoons onions, chopped
- 2 tablespoons celery, chopped (optional)
- Salt to taste

Method:
1. Mix together all the ingredients in a bowl.
2. Toss well and cover with cling wrap. For a change in taste, omit sweet pickle relish and add some mayonnaise or any other dressing of your choice.
3. Chill until use. It can last for up to 2 days.

Avocado Cashew Salad

Serves: 2

Ingredients:
- 2 small avocadoes, peeled, pitted, chopped
- 1 large tomato, chopped or 1 cup cherry tomatoes, halved
- ½ cup cashews, chopped
- Salt to taste
- Pepper to taste
- Juice of a lime

Method:
1. Mix together all the ingredients except salt in a bowl.
2. Place in the refrigerator until use.
3. To serve: Add salt. Toss well and serve.

Chicken and Avocado Caesar Salad

Serves: 3
Cook time: 10 minutes

Ingredients:

For salad:
- 3 chicken breasts, skinless, boneless
- 2 heads Romaine lettuce, torn
- 6 slices bacon, cooked, crumbled
- 1 large avocado, peeled, pitted, sliced
- 3 eggs, boiled, sliced
- 2 teaspoons garlic powder
- 3 teaspoons dried oregano
- 2 teaspoons chili powder or to taste
- Sea salt to taste
- Freshly ground black pepper to taste

For Caesar dressing:
- 1 ½ cups mayonnaise
- 3 tablespoons fresh lemon juice
- 3 cloves garlic, minced
- 1 ½ teaspoons Dijon mustard
- 3 teaspoons anchovy paste
- Sea salt to taste
- Freshly ground black pepper to taste

Method:
1. Mix together in a small bowl, chili powder, garlic powder, oregano, salt and pepper. Rub this mixture on the chicken breasts.
2. Grill the chicken breasts in a preheated grill (medium high heat) until done.
3. Remove from the grill and place on your cutting board. When cool enough to handle, slice the chicken. Transfer into an airtight container and refrigerate until use.
4. To make dressing: Add all the ingredients of the dressing to a bowl and whisk well. Cover and refrigerate until use.
5. To serve: Add lettuce, bacon and avocado into a bowl and toss well. Divide this mixture into individual serving bowls.

6. Warm the chicken slices in a microwave or in an oven. Place chicken slices and egg slices over it.
7. Pour Caesar dressing on top and serve.

Cabbage Orange Salad

Serves: 2

Ingredients:

- 2 oranges, peeled, sliced into ½ inch segments, deseeded
- 1 head purple cabbage, thinly sliced
- 2 tablespoons olive oil
- 2 tablespoons lemon juice
- 2 tablespoons apple cider vinegar
- Chili powder to taste
- Salt to taste

Method:

1. Place cabbage and orange segments in a large bowl. Refrigerate until use.
2. Add olive oil, vinegar, salt, and chili powder and lemon juice into a small bowl. Whisk well.
3. It can last for 2 days if refrigerated.
4. To serve: Pour dressing over the salad. Toss well and serve.

Fattoush

Serves: 2
Cook time: 15 minutes

Ingredients:
- 1 (6-inch) whole-wheat pita bread, split
- 1 ½ tablespoons extra-virgin olive oil, divided
- ¾ teaspoon ground sumac, divided
- 2 tablespoons lemon juice
- 1/4 teaspoon salt or to taste
- Freshly ground pepper to taste
- 1 medium head romaine lettuce, coarsely chopped
- 1 large tomato, diced
- 1 small salad cucumber, diced
- ¼ cup red onions, thinly sliced
- 1 tablespoon fresh mint, thinly chopped

Method:
1. Place the pita halves on a baking sheet with the rough side up. Brush with ½ tablespoon olive oil and sprinkle half the sumac.
2. Bake in a preheated oven at 350° F for about 15 minutes or until crisp and golden. Remove from the oven. When cool, chop into bite size pieces. Transfer into an airtight container.
3. Mix together tomato, lettuce, onions, cucumber and mint in a large bowl. Refrigerate until use. It can last for 2 days.
4. In a glass bowl add lemon juice, salt, pepper, remaining oil, and sumac. Whisk well refrigerate until use.
5. To serve: Remove the salad and dressing from the refrigerator 30 minutes before your meal. Add the pita pieces to the salad bowl. Pour dressing on top.
6. Toss well to coat.
7. Serve after 15 minutes.

Kale and Avocado Salad with Almonds

Serves: 2

Ingredients:

- 1 ripe avocado, peeled, pitted, chopped
- 1 bunch kale, discard hard ribs and stems, rinsed, torn
- 2 cloves garlic, minced
- 2 apples, cored, diced
- ½ cup almonds, toasted to golden brown
- 1 teaspoon sea salt or to taste
- 4 tablespoons olive oil
- 2 sheets of nori

Method:

1. Mix together avocado, kale, garlic, salt and olive oil and massage it well with your hands for a couple of minutes. The kale should become smaller in size due to massaging. Add apple and almonds. Chill until use.
2. Using tongs, lightly roast the nori sheets directly over a gas burner for a couple of seconds so that it becomes softer and bright green in color. Quarter them and cut into thin strips.
3. Place the salad in individual serving bowls. Place the nori strips and serve.

Salsa Salad

Serves: 3

Ingredients:
- 2 tablespoons olive oil
- 1 large onion, finely chopped
- 1 red bell pepper, chopped
- 1 green bell pepper, chopped
- 3 tablespoons lime juice
- 1 ½ cups fresh cilantro, chopped
- 2 chili peppers, finely chopped
- 6 Roma tomatoes, chopped
- 2 green onions thinly sliced
- 1 large avocado, peeled, pitted, cubed
- Sea salt to taste

Method:
1. Mix together all the ingredients in a large bowl.
2. Toss well.
3. Chill until use. It can last for up to 2 days.

Chicken Waldorf salad

Ingredients:
- 1 ½ cups chicken
- 2 stalks celery, trimmed, chopped
- 1 apple, cored, chopped into chunks
- 10 almonds
- Mayonnaise as required
- 1 tablespoon lemon juice

Method:
1. Cook the chicken. Transfer into a container. Add rest of the ingredients to it and toss. Cover and refrigerate until use.
2. It can last for 2-3 days.

Chapter 9: Soup Recipes

Chilled Avocado Soup

Serves: 6

Ingredients:
- 3 cups Hass avocado puree
- 3 cups vegetable broth
- 1 cup coconut cream (optional)
- ½ cup cilantro, chopped
- 2 jalapeno peppers, deseeded, chopped
- 2 teaspoons ground cumin
- 1 teaspoon salt or to taste

Method:
1. Add all the ingredients into a food processor and blend until smooth.
2. Transfer into a bowl. Cover and chill until use. It can last for 2-3 days.
3. Serve in individual bowls.

Summer Vegetable Soup

Serves: 6-8

Ingredients:
- 4 cups fat free, plain yogurt
- 1 cup cilantro, chopped
- 8 large tomatoes, diced into 1 inch pieces
- 2 large red bell peppers, diced into ½ inch pieces
- 2 large cucumbers, peeled, deseeded, sliced
- 2 large onions, chopped
- 6 cups tomato juice, low sodium
- ½ cup red wine vinegar
- 4 teaspoons red pepper sauce or to taste
- ½ teaspoon black pepper powder
- 2 cloves garlic, minced

Method:
1. Mix together 1-cup yogurt and cilantro, set aside.
2. Blend together half of each- tomatoes, bell pepper, cucumber, onions, and the remaining yogurt. Blend until smooth.
3. Add the tomato juice, vinegar, pepper sauce, garlic, and pepper powder and blend until smooth.
4. Add the remaining half of the chopped vegetables and stir. Chill until use. It can last for up to 3-4 days.
5. Serve in individual soup bowls. Top with the cilantro – yogurt mixture.

Seafood Gazpacho

Serves: 6

Ingredients:
- 1 pound bay scallops, rinsed, pat dried
- ½ pound shrimp, cooked, rinsed, pat dried
- 1 large yellow bell pepper, diced into 1/4 inch pieces
- 1 medium onion, minced
- 2 medium tomatoes, deseeded, chopped
- 1 1/3 cups cucumber, chopped
- 6 cloves garlic, peeled, pressed
- 4 tablespoons extra virgin olive oil
- 2 cans (4 ounce each) diced green chili
- 6 cups tomato juice
- Salt to taste
- Freshly cracked pepper to taste
- ½ cup lemon juice
- ½ cup fresh cilantro, chopped

Method:
1. Pour lemon juice over the scallops and set aside. If you don't like your scallops raw, then steam for just a minute and then marinate in lemon juice.
2. Add rest of the ingredients in a bowl and mix well. Let it sit for a while for the flavors to set in.
3. Add scallops to it. Mix well and chill until use. It can last for up to 2-3 days.
4. Serve chilled in soup bowls.

Summer Fruit Soup

Serves: 4
Cook time: 8 minutes

Ingredients:
- 1 ½ cups strawberries, chopped
- ½ cup raspberries
- ½ tablespoon minced ginger
- ¾ cup mango, chopped
- 1 cup pineapple, chopped
- ¼ teaspoon lime zest
- ¼ teaspoon lemon zest
- 2 cups water
- ¼ teaspoon orange peel
- Agave nectar to taste (optional)
- ¼ cup fresh orange juice
- 1 tablespoon fresh lime juice
- 1 tablespoon fresh lemon juice
- ½ cup blueberries
- 1 ripe peach, seeded, chopped
- 1 cup canned peach nectar
- Ice cubes
- Mint sprigs, to garnish
- A few raspberries and blue berries to garnish

Method:
1. Place a large saucepan over medium heat. Add ginger and sauté until fragrant. Add ½ the strawberries, pineapple, and mango, lime zest, lemon zest and orange zest.
2. Mix well and sauté for a couple of minutes. Add water, sugar, orange juice, lemon juice and lime juice. Cook for 3-4 minutes. Remove from heat and cool.
3. Transfer the contents into a blender. Add the remaining ½ strawberries, pineapple, and mango, ½ the blueberries and raspberries, peach, peach nectar, and ice. Blend until smooth.
4. Pour into bowls and garnish with mint sprigs, raspberries, and blueberries.
5. Chill until use. It can last for 2-3 days.

Strawberry Cantaloupe Soup

Serves: 2

Ingredients:
- 2 cups ripe cantaloupe, peeled, seeded, cubed
- 1 cup ripe strawberries, hulled
- ¾ cup fresh orange juice
- ¾ cup dry white wine
- 1 tablespoon fresh lime juice
- ½ teaspoon ginger, minced
- 2 tablespoons fresh mint, minced
- Sliced strawberries and mint leaves for garnishing

Method:
1. Blend together all the ingredients except mint in a blender until smooth.
2. Add mint. Mix well and refrigerate.
3. Ladle into soup bowls. Garnish with sliced strawberries and mint leaves and chill until use. It can last for 2-3 days.

Gazpacho

Serves: 6

Ingredients:
- 2 red onions, finely chopped
- 6 tomatoes, finely chopped
- 1 medium cucumber, finely chopped
- 1 green pepper, deseeded, finely chopped
- 6 stalks of celery, finely chopped
- 1 garlic clove, crushed
- 7 cups tomato juice
- ½ cup extra virgin olive oil
- ½ cup white wine vinegar
- ½ cup fresh parsley, finely chopped
- ½ teaspoon white powdered stevia
- Salt to taste
- Pepper to taste

Method:
1. Mix together all the ingredients in a bowl. Cover and chill in the refrigerator until use. It can last for 2 days.
2. Serve in individual soup bowls.

Kale Soup

Serves: 8
Cook time: 25 minutes

Ingredients:
- 1 large onion, chopped
- 2 carrots, peeled, cubed
- 4 red potatoes, rinsed, scrubbed, cubed
- 6 cups kale, hard ribs and stems discarded, finely sliced
- 5 stalks celery, chopped
- 10 cups vegetable stock
- 4 teaspoons dried sage
- 4 teaspoons dried thyme
- Salt to taste
- Pepper powder to taste

Method:
1. Place a large saucepan over medium heat. Add about a tablespoon of broth. Add onions and sauté until onions are translucent. Add garlic and sauté for a couple of minutes.
2. Add rest of the ingredients except kale and bring to the boil.
3. Lower heat and cover.
4. Simmer until tender.
5. Add kale and cook for a few minutes until kale wilts. Cool and transfer into an airtight container. It can last for 2-3 days if refrigerated.
6. Heat thoroughly and serve when required.

Tofu Noodle Soup

Serves: 8
Cook time: 25 minutes

Ingredients:

- 9 cups water
- 3 cups tofu, chopped
- 3 carrots, peeled, chopped
- 12 green beans, chopped into ½ cm pieces
- 1 green bell pepper, chopped
- 1 red bell pepper, chopped
- 2 ½ cups cabbage, chopped
- 1 ½ cups fresh or frozen corn
- ½ cup parsley, chopped
- 5 stalks celery, chopped
- 10 tablespoons vegetarian broth powder
- 1 ½ teaspoons sea salt or Himalayan salt
- 1 teaspoon pepper powder
- A dash of hot sauce to serve
- ¾ box quinoa spaghetti noodles, broken into 2 inch pieces

Method:

1. Add all the ingredients except noodles to a soup pot or large saucepan. Place the saucepan over medium heat. Bring to the boil.
2. Lower heat and cover.
3. Simmer until the vegetables are tender. Remove from heat and cool completely.
4. Add noodles and cook until the noodles are al dente. Transfer soup into an airtight container. Also add the noodles and stir. Cover and chill until use. It can last for up to 2 days.
5. Heat thoroughly before use. Ladle into individual soup bowls. Add a dash of hot sauce and serve immediately.

Creamy Radish Soup

Serves: 4
Cook time: 25 minutes

Ingredients:

- 4 cup radish, sliced, divided
- 2 medium Yukon gold potatoes, peeled, chopped into 1 inch cubes
- 1 cup onions, chopped
- 4 tablespoons extra virgin olive oil
- ½ cup low fat sour cream
- Salt to taste
- White or black pepper to taste
- 4 cups low fat milk
- 2 tablespoons fresh radish greens, chopped to serve

Method:

1. Slice about ½ cup of radish into matchsticks and refrigerate until use.
2. Place a large saucepan over medium high heat. Add oil. When the oil is heated, add 3 ½ cups radish and onion and sauté until the onions are brown and radish are slightly soft.
3. Add potatoes, salt, pepper and milk and bring to the boil. Stir a couple of times.
4. Lower heat and cover. Simmer until the potatoes are tender. Remove from heat.
5. Cool slightly. Blend the contents with an immersion blender until smooth.
6. Heat thoroughly. Remove from heat. Cool completely. Transfer into a container and refrigerate until use. Can last for up to 2 days
7. Heat thoroughly before use. Ladle into individual soup bowls. Place some of the matchstick radish in each bowl. Garnish with about a tablespoon of sour cream in each bowl. Sprinkle radish greens on top and serve.

Cream of Zucchini Soup

Serves: 6
Cook time: 15 minutes

Ingredients:

- 5 medium zucchinis, chopped into chunks
- 2 onions, quartered
- 6 cups vegetable stock or chicken stock
- 4 cloves garlic, sliced
- ¼ cup coconut milk or low fat milk or any other milk of your choice
- 1 tablespoon ghee or coconut oil
- Freshly ground black pepper to taste
- Sea salt to taste

Method:

1. Place a saucepan over medium heat. Add coconut oil. When the oil melts, add onions, garlic and sauté for a few minutes until translucent.
2. Add zucchinis and sauté for 4-5 minutes.
3. Add stock, salt and pepper and bring to a boil.
4. Reduce heat and simmer until the vegetables are tender.
5. Remove from heat and add coconut milk. Blend the contents with an immersion blender or in a blender until smooth.
6. Taste and adjust the seasonings. Transfer into an airtight container and refrigerator until use.
7. Heat thoroughly before use. Ladle into individual soup bowls and serve.

Split Pea Soup

Serves: 3
Cook time: 75 minutes

Ingredients:

- ¾ cup green/yellow split peas, rinsed, soaked in water overnight, drained
- ½ pound extra lean ground turkey
- 1 medium carrot, diced
- 1 medium onion, minced
- 1 bay leaf
- 3 cups water
- ½ teaspoon liquid smoke
- Freshly ground black pepper to taste
- Salt to taste
- Cooking spray

Method:

1. Place split peas in a pot. Place the pot over medium heat. Add water and bay leaf and bring to the boil.
2. Lower heat and cover.
3. Simmer until tender. It will take about 45 minutes.
4. Meanwhile, place a skillet over medium heat. Spray with cooking spray. Add onions and sauté until soft. Remove the onions and set aside in a bowl.
5. Place the skillet back over heat. Add turkey and sauté until golden brown. Break it simultaneously as it cooks.
6. Once the split peas are tender, add the onions that were set aside, carrots, salt, pepper and liquid smoke.
7. Cover and cook until the carrots are tender. Discard the bay leaf. Cool completely and transfer into an airtight container. Can last for 4 days if refrigerated and 3 months if frozen.
8. Heat thoroughly before use. Ladle into individual soup bowls. Serve with sprouted, toasted bread.

Thai Chicken Soup

Serves: 3
Cook time: 35 minutes

Ingredients:
- 1 chicken breasts, skinless, boneless, cut into thin strips
- 4 scallions, chopped
- 2 teaspoons Thai red curry paste
- ½ cup coconut milk
- 3 cups chicken broth
- 1 ½ teaspoons ground coriander
- 2 teaspoons lemon juice
- 2 teaspoons lime juice
- ½ teaspoon fish sauce
- 1 teaspoon salt or to taste
- 1 tablespoon fresh ginger or galangal, peeled, minced
- 2 tablespoons fresh cilantro, chopped

Method:
1. Place a large skillet over medium heat.
2. Add broth, chicken, lemon juice, and ginger and bring to a boil.
3. Lower heat and cover. Simmer for 20 minutes.
4. Add rest of the ingredients except cilantro and simmer for 10 minutes. Cool and transfer into an airtight container. Can last for 3-4 days if refrigerated and can last for 2 months if frozen.
5. Heat thoroughly before use. Ladle into individual soup bowls. Garnish with cilantro and serve.

Chicken and Spinach Soup with Fresh Pesto

Serves: 3
Cook time: 25 minutes

Ingredients:

- 3 teaspoons extra virgin olive oil, divided
- 1 medium carrot, chopped
- 1 red bell pepper, chopped
- 5 ounces chicken breast, skinless, boneless, quartered
- 3 cups low sodium chicken broth
- 1 clove garlic, minced
- 1 teaspoon dried marjoram
- 9 ounces canned cannellini beans or great northern beans, rinsed
- 4 ounces baby spinach, chopped
- ½ cup fresh basil leaves, chopped
- 3 tablespoons parmesan, grated
- Freshly ground pepper to taste
- Salt to taste
- Multigrain croutons to serve

Method:

1. Place a saucepan over medium high heat. Add 1-teaspoon oil. When the oil is heated, add carrot, bell pepper, and chicken and sauté until the chicken is brown. Add garlic and sauté until fragrant.
2. Add broth and marjoram and bring to the boil.
3. Lower heat and cover. Simmer until chicken is tender. Remove the chicken with a slotted spoon and place on your work area. When cool enough to handle, chop into bite size pieces.
4. Meanwhile, add spinach and beans into the saucepan and cook until the spinach wilts.
5. To make pesto: Add remaining oil into the blender. Also add Parmesan and basil and pulse until you get a coarse texture. Add a little water and pulse again. Transfer into the saucepan. Also add chicken and pepper. Heat thoroughly. Cool and refrigerate until use. Can last for 3-4 days if refrigerated and 2-3 months if frozen.
6. Thaw if frozen. Heat thoroughly before use. Ladle into individual soup bowls.
7. Top with croutons and serve.

Chapter 10: Snack/Appetizer Recipes

Kale Chips

Serves: 4
Cook time: 12-15 minutes

Ingredients:
- 2-3 bunches of kale leaves, discard hard stem and ribs, rinsed, drained, dried, torn
- Cooking spray
- Salt to taste
- Red chili flakes to taste (optional)
- Any seasoning of your choice (optional)

Method:
1. Sprinkle salt and chili on kale. Sprinkle the seasoning if using. Spray with cooking spray. Keep aside for a while.
2. Spread the leaves on a baking sheet.
3. Bake in a preheated oven at 250° F for about 10 minutes until crisp and done. Cool and vacuum seal in plastic to store for longer time. For a short duration, store in paper bags. Do not refrigerate. If by chance the chips have got some moisture in it and have lost its crispiness, then bake for minutes. Cool completely.
4. Note: You can make zucchini chips or sweet potato chips in similar manner by replacing kale leaves with thin slices of zucchini or sweet potatoes.

Crispy Edamame Popcorn

Serves: 2
Cook time: 45 minutes

Ingredients:
- 6 ounces frozen edamame, shelled, thawed
- 1 teaspoon lemon juice
- 1 teaspoon olive oil
- Salt to taste
- Any seasoning of your choice (optional)

Method:
1. Place edamame in a bowl. Add oil and lemon juice.
2. Place in a foil lined baking sheet and bake in a preheated oven at 375° F for about 45 minutes or until light brown and crisp.
3. Remove from oven and sprinkle salt immediately. Sprinkle seasoning if using. Cool completely and store in an airtight container. It can last for 3-4 days.

Chili -Lime Spiced Pumpkin Seeds

Serves: 12
Cook time 15 minutes

Ingredients:
- 6 cups raw pumpkin seeds (pepitas)
- 2 tablespoons butter or ghee, melted (optional)
- 2 teaspoons cayenne pepper
- 2 teaspoons chili powder or to taste
- 1 ½ teaspoons sea salt
- 1/3 cup fresh lemon juice

Method:
1. Place the pepitas in a baking dish. Add ghee, lemon juice, cayenne pepper, chili powder, sea salt and cayenne pepper and toss well.
2. Bake in a preheated oven at 275° F for about 10-15 minutes or until done. Cool and store in an airtight container until use. It can last for 10 days.
3. You can make variations by adding a seasoning of your choice.
4. You can also make spicy nuts using the same ingredients replacing pumpkin seeds with nuts of your choice.

Veggie Lettuce Wraps

Serves: 8

Ingredients:
- 8 leaves iceberg lettuce
- 1 large carrot, cut into matchsticks
- ½ cucumber, cut into matchsticks
- Mayonnaise as required
- ¼ teaspoon paprika

Method:
1. Spread lettuce leaves on your work area.
2. Place carrots and cucumber matchsticks over the leaves. Add a dollop of mayonnaise. Sprinkle paprika.
3. Roll and fix a toothpick on it. Place in a container. Cover and refrigerate until use. It can be stored for 2 days.

Spinach Hummus Pinwheel Wraps

Serves: 4

Ingredients:
- 2 whole grain tortillas
- 2 cups packed spinach, steamed
- 1 small red bell pepper, thinly sliced
- A few thin cucumber slices
- 1 clove garlic, peeled
- 7.5 ounces canned unsalted cannellini beans
- ½ avocado, peeled, pitted, thinly sliced
- 2 tablespoons low sodium vegetable broth or water
- 1 tablespoon tahini
- 1 tablespoon lemon juice
- ¼ teaspoon salt or to taste

Method:
1. To make spinach hummus: Add spinach, beans, lemon juice, tahini, garlic and salt to a food processor and pulse until smooth.
2. Place tortilla on your work area. Apply spinach hummus over it. Lay avocado, cucumber and bell pepper slices. Roll tightly and set-aside in an airtight container in the refrigerator until use.
3. To serve, warm for 20 seconds in a microwave. Chop into ¾ inch pinwheels and serve.

Chicken Fingers

Serves: 12
Cook time: 20 minutes

Ingredients:
- 4 chicken breasts, chop into strips of about 1 inch wide and 3 inches long
- 4 tablespoons curry powder or to taste
- 1 ¼ cups coconut flour
- 3 teaspoons garlic powder
- 1 teaspoon turmeric powder
- 3 teaspoons cumin powder
- Salt to taste

Method:
1. Mix together all the dry ingredients in a bowl.
2. Dredge the chicken pieces in the dry mixture. Shake off the excess mixture and place on a greased baking dish. Cover with foil and refrigerate until use.
3. Remove from the refrigerator and thaw for 30 minutes.
4. Bake in a preheated oven at 350° F for 20 minutes or until done.

Fish Sticks

Serves: 8
Cook time: 15 minutes

Ingredients:
- 2 pounds white fish like cod or snapper or tilapia, rinsed, chopped into 1 inch by 5 inch sticks
- 2 cups blanched almond flour
- 4 large eggs, whisked
- 2 teaspoons sea salt or to taste
- 2/3 cup olive oil or coconut oil

Method:
1. Place almond flour and salt in a wide, shallow dish and mix well. Place eggs in another wide shallow dish.
2. First dip the fish sticks in the egg and then dredge in the flour mixture and place in an airtight container.
3. Place a large skillet over medium high heat. Add about 3 tablespoons oil. Add about ¼ the fish sticks (do not over crowd) and cook until the bottom side is brown. Flip sides and cook the other side too. Remove and place on a plate lined with paper towels.
4. Repeat the above step with the remaining fish sticks.
5. Store fish sticks in an airtight container in the refrigerator for 4-5 days. To heat, place fish sticks on the wire rack in an oven.
6. Bake in a preheated oven at 350° F for 20 minutes or until done.
5. Serve with a dip of your choice.

Pita Pizza

Serves: 12
Cook time: 30 minutes

Ingredients:

For Pizza:
- 2 whole wheat pita breads (7 ½ inches each)
- 1 ½ ounces mozzarella cheese, grated
- ½ a yellow bell pepper, deseeded, chop into thin strips

For tomato sauce:
- 1 yellow onion, peeled, chopped into 1 cm pieces
- 1 small bay leaf
- 7 ounces canned whole tomatoes, peeled, chopped
- ½ teaspoon olive oil
- 1 clove garlic, peeled, minced
- ¼ teaspoon dried basil
- ¼ teaspoon dried oregano
- ¼ teaspoon crushed red pepper flakes
- Salt to taste
- 2 tablespoons tomato paste

Method:

1. To make tomato sauce: Place a pan over medium heat. Add oil. When oil is heated, add onion and garlic and sauté until brown.
2. Add oregano, basil, bay leaf, red pepper flakes, tomatoes and tomato paste.
3. Mix well and bring to a boil.
4. Lower heat to medium low and cover.
5. Let it simmer for a while until the liquid is dried up.
6. Place pita bread on a baking sheet. Divide and spread tomato sauce over it. Sprinkle bell pepper strips followed by mozzarella cheese. Carefully place in an airtight container in the refrigerator until use. Thaw before use. It can last for 3-4 days.
7. Bake in a preheated oven at 350° F for about 20 minutes or until the cheese melts.
8. Remove the pizzas from the oven and transfer on to your work area. Garnish with basil and cut each pizza into 12 wedges and serve.

Guacamole Devilled Eggs

Serves: 8
Cook time: 10 minutes

Ingredients:
- 8 hard-boiled eggs, peeled
- 3 tablespoons guacamole
- 1 teaspoon lemon juice
- Sea salt to taste
- Pepper powder to taste
- 1 teaspoon hot pepper sauce

Method:
1. Halve the eggs lengthwise. Scoop out the yolks and place in a bowl. Place the whites on a plate.
2. Add rest of the ingredients to the bowl. Divide the mixture into 16 portions. Stuff this mixture into the cavity of the eggs and place in an airtight container.
3. Refrigerate until use. It can last for 2-3 days.

Chapter 11: Main Course Recipes

Curried Chicken over Spinach

Serves: 4
Cook time: 20 minutes

Ingredients:
- 2 chicken breasts, boneless, skinless, chopped into bite sized pieces
- 1 small onion, halved, sliced
- 1 cup chicken stock
- 1 small red bell pepper, thinly sliced
- 3 bunches fresh spinach, rinsed
- ½ tablespoons fresh ginger, minced
- 2 cloves garlic, sliced
- 1 teaspoon curry powder
- ¼ teaspoon turmeric powder
- 6 tablespoons coconut milk
- White pepper powder to taste
- Salt to taste

Method:
1. Place a nonstick pan over medium low heat. Add onions and sauté for 5 minutes.
2. Add ginger and garlic and sauté for a couple of minutes until fragrant.
3. Add turmeric and curry powder and sauté for a few seconds.
4. Add stock, chicken, coconut milk and simmer for 5-6 minutes. Add bell pepper and cook until the chicken is tender. Remove from heat and cool. Transfer into a container. Cover and refrigerate until use.
5. To serve: Boil a pot of water and add spinach to it. Boil for a minute and drain. Press to squeeze out the excess moisture. Sprinkle salt and pepper and set aside. Heat chicken curry.
6. Place blanched spinach on serving plates and place chicken mixture over it.
7. Serve with brown rice.

Chicken Parmesan

Serves: 2
Cook time: 40 minutes

Ingredients:
- 2 chicken breasts, skinless, trimmed
- 2 tablespoons arrowroot flour
- ½ cup almond flour
- 2 eggs, beaten
- ¼ teaspoon onion powder
- ½ teaspoon oregano
- ¼ teaspoon garlic powder
- ½ teaspoon basil
- Salt to taste
- Pepper to taste
- Crushed red pepper flakes to taste
- Spaghetti sauce as required
- 1 cup parmesan cheese, shredded

Method:
1. Add flours, spices herbs and salt into a bowl. Mix well.
2. First dip a chicken breast into the egg. Shake off excess egg. Next dredge the chicken into the flour mixture. Dip again into the egg and dredge in the flour. Place on a lined baking sheet.
3. Repeat the above step with the other chicken breast.
4. Bake in a preheated oven at 375° F for about 40 minutes.
5. Cool.
6. Line a freezable baking dish with plastic wrap with extra hanging from the sides. Spread some spaghetti sauce at the bottom of the dish. Place chicken over it.
7. Top with spaghetti sauce. Sprinkle Parmesan over it. Cover and freeze for a few hours.
8. When it is frozen, pull the chicken with the help of the plastic wrap from the dish. Cover with the extra wrap. Wrap some more plastic wrap over it and label it. Place in the freezer until use.
9. To use: Remove from the freezer. Peel off the plastic wrap and place in a baking dish. Thaw if desired.
10. Bake until thoroughly heated and serve with brown rice noodles or zucchini noodles.

Chicken Taco Pizza

Serves: 8
Cook time: 30 minutes

Ingredients:
- 2 whole wheat pizza crusts, freshly made or frozen
- 2 frozen chicken breasts, skinless, boneless, thawed, chopped into bite sized pieces
- 2 cups frozen corn, thawed
- 2 cups cooked black beans, rinsed, drained
- 1 cup salsa + extra to serve
- 2 cups part skim mozzarella cheese, grated, divided
- ½ cup fresh cilantro, chopped

Method:
1. Lay the pizza crusts on a large baking sheet. Divide salsa and spread over both the crusts. Sprinkle half the cheese over the salsa.
2. Sprinkle beans, corn, and chicken over the cheese. Finally top with the remaining cheese.
3. Bake in a preheated oven 425° F until slightly brown.
4. Remove from the oven and cool. Sprinkle cheese over it. Sprinkle cilantro on it. Refrigerate until use. It can last for 2-3 days.
5. To serve: Bake in a preheated oven for 10-15 minutes or until the cheese is melted and light brown in color.
6. Cut into wedges and serve with some salsa.

Chicken Paprika

Serves: 6
Cook time:

Ingredients:
- 6 chicken breasts, skinless, boneless, chop into chunks
- 4 tablespoons olive oil
- 4 tablespoons Spanish smoked paprika
- 3 tablespoons lemon juice
- 1 ½ tablespoons maple syrup
- 3 teaspoons garlic, minced
- Salt to taste
- Pepper powder to taste

Method:
1. Mix together all the ingredients except the chicken to make the sauce.
2. Season the chicken with salt and pepper.
3. Pour 1/3 of the sauce to a casserole dish. Place the chicken pieces on top of it.
4. Pour the remaining sauce all over the chicken pieces.
5. Bake in a preheated oven at 350° F for about 30 minutes or until done. When cooled, transfer into an airtight container freezer safe container. It can last for 4 days if refrigerated or up to 2 months if frozen.
6. Bake until thoroughly heated and serve.

Coconut Shrimp and Avocadoes

Serves: 2
Cook time: 10-12 minutes

Ingredients:
- 1 avocado, peeled, pitted, chop into bite sized cubes
- 2 cups shrimp
- 2 teaspoons Sriracha sauce or any other hot sauce
- 1 tablespoon natural peanut butter
- 2 teaspoons shredded coconut
- 2 tablespoons light coconut milk
- Salt to taste
- Cooking spray

Method:
1. Place a nonstick pan over medium heat. Spray with cooking spray.
2. Add coconut milk, peanut butter, salt and hot sauce. Stir until well combined.
3. Add shrimp and cook until shrimp are tender.
4. Remove from heat and sprinkle coconut over it. Cool and transfer into a container. Cover and refrigerate until use. It can last for 2-3 days.
5. To serve: Heat the shrimp. Place avocadoes on a serving plate. Place the shrimp over it and serve.

Seared Salmon in Green Peppercorn Sauce

Serves: 6
Cook time: 10 minutes

Ingredients:
- 2 ½ pounds wild salmon fillet, skinned, cut into big pieces
- ½ cup lemon juice
- 4 teaspoons canola oil
- ½ teaspoon salt, divided
- 3 tablespoons unsalted butter, chopped coarsely
- 2 teaspoons green peppercorns soaked in vinegar

Method:
1. Season salmon pieces with half the salt.
2. Place a large nonstick skillet over medium high heat. Add half the oil.
3. Add half the salmon pieces and cook for 2-3 minutes and flip sides. Cook until the salmon pieces turn opaque in the center.
4. Repeat step 2 and 3 with the remaining salmon pieces.
5. When done add the first batch of seared salmon back to the pan. Stir for a minute and remove from heat. Transfer into a baking dish. Cover and refrigerate until use. It can last for 3-4 days.
6. Add lemon juice, peppercorns (rinse and crush them before using), butter, and remaining salt. Then swirl the pan so that butter melts and peppercorn are well blended in the butter.
7. To serve: Heat the salmon. Place salmon pieces on individual plates and pour sauce over it and serve.

Easy Tuna Sliders

Serves: 4

Ingredients:
- 2 cans wild albacore tuna
- 2 large cucumbers
- 4 tablespoons spicy mustard
- 2 tablespoons apple cider vinegar
- Salt to taste
- Pepper to taste

Method:
1. Cut the cucumber into around 1/3-inch slices. Drizzle apple cider vinegar on the cucumber and set aside for a while.
2. Mix together tuna and mustard in a bowl.
3. Place cucumber slices on a serving platter. Top each slice with the tuna mixture. Place in a container. Cover and refrigerate until use. It can last for 2 days.
4. Season with salt and pepper and serve at room temperature.

Shrimp and Bacon skillet

Serves: 8
Cook time: 10 minutes

Ingredients:
- 8 slices uncured bacon, cut into 1 inch pieces
- 2 cups mushrooms, sliced
- 8 ounces smoked salmon, cut into strips
- 8 ounces raw shelled shrimp
- 1 cup coconut cream
- A large pinch Celtic sea salt or to taste
- Freshly ground black pepper to taste

Method:
1. Place a large cast iron skillet over medium heat. Add bacon. Cook until done.
2. Add mushrooms and sauté until tender.
3. Add smoked salmon. Sauté for 2-3 minutes.
4. Add coconut cream and salt. Reduce heat and simmer for a minute. Remove from heat and cool. Cover and refrigerate until use.
5. To serve: Remove skillet from refrigerator and place over medium heat. Heat thoroughly.
6. Serve immediately with zucchini noodles.

Grilled Teriyaki Pork Lettuce Wraps

Serves: 8
Cook time: 12 minutes

Ingredients:
- 1 pork tenderloin of about 2 pounds
- 2 heads Boston Lettuce, separate leaves, rinse, pat dry
- 2/3 cup teriyaki sauce + extra for serving
- 1 cup carrots, peeled, shredded
- 1 cup radish, shredded
- 1 cup cucumber, shredded
- 1 cup Napa cabbage, shredded
- 1 cup mixed fresh herbs of your choice, chopped

Method:
1. Place pork in a bowl and pour teriyaki sauce over it. Coat well and marinate for at least a couple of hours in the refrigerator.
2. Preheat a grill to medium high. Carefully remove the pork from the bowl discarding the remaining marinade and place on the grill.
3. Grill until brown and done. This should take around 10-12 minutes. Turn pork frequently. If you think that the pork is getting brown and not getting cooked inside, and then move the pork to a comparatively cooler part of the grill.
4. When done, place the pork on your cutting board. When cool enough to handle, slice it into thin strips.
5. Place lettuce leaves on your work area.
6. Sprinkle vegetables over the leaves. Place pork strips over it. Sprinkle mixed herbs. Drizzle some teriyaki sauce over it. Wrap and place in a container. Cover and refrigerate until use. It can last for 2 days.
7. Serve at room temperature.

Sausage and Cauliflower Bake

Serves: 8
Cook time: 40 minutes

Ingredients:

- 1 Large cauliflower, chopped into florets
- 8 pork sausages
- 10 tablespoons coconut cream
- 8 slices low fat cheese or non dairy cheese
- 1 teaspoon salt or to taste
- Pepper powder to taste

Method:

1. Steam the cauliflower florets. Mash with a potato masher.
2. Add coconut cream, salt and pepper.
3. Place a nonstick skillet over medium heat. Add sausages and cook until done.
4. When cool enough to handle, slice the sausages and add to cauliflower mixture and mix well.
5. Now layer as follows:
6. Add half the cauliflower mixture to a greased freezer safe baking dish.
7. Lay half the cheese slices.
8. Spread the remaining mixture over the cheese slices.
9. Lay the remaining cheese slices over the cauliflower layer. It can last for 3-4 days if refrigerated or up to 2 months if frozen.
10. Place the baking dish in a in a preheated oven and bake at 350° F for around 30 minutes. Preferably thaw before baking.

Pulled Pork Poblano

Serves: 4
Cook time: 2 hours

Ingredients:

- 1 ½ pounds pork shoulder, trimmed of fat, chopped into 2 inch chunks
- ½ pound tomatillos, husked, quartered
- 1 Serrano pepper, halved, sliced
- 1 poblano pepper or more if you like it hot, deseeded, halved, sliced
- 1 small onion, chopped
- 1 teaspoon safflower oil
- Pepper to taste
- Salt to taste
- 3 cloves garlic, smashed
- ½ teaspoon ground coriander
- 1 ½ teaspoons ground cumin
- Juice of ½ lime
- 2 cups chicken broth

Method:

1. Place a heavy bottomed heatproof pot or Dutch oven over high heat. Add oil. When the oil is heated, add pork and sprinkle salt and pepper over it. Cook until brown.
2. Remove pork with a slotted spoon and set aside. Discard the fat that is remaining in the pot.
3. Place the pot back on heat. Add tomatillos, onion, garlic and peppers and sauté until brown.
4. Add spices, salt and pepper and sauté for a few seconds until fragrant. Add broth and the pork along with the released juices into the pot. Add more broth if required. The pork should be covered with broth.
5. Bring to the boil.
6. Lower heat and cover. Simmer until the pork is tender. It may take 1 ½ - 2 hours.
7. Remove the pork with a slotted spoon and place on your work area. When cool enough to handle, shred with a pair of forks.
8. Meanwhile, remove any fat that is floating on the top. Simmer the liquid until thick. Add lime juice, salt and pepper if necessary.
9. Add the pork back into the pot and mix. Transfer into a container. Cover and refrigerate until use. It can last for 4 days.
10. Heat thoroughly and serve.

Coconut Red Pork Curry

Serves: 4
Cook time: 20 minutes

Ingredients:
- 1 ½ pounds pork tenderloin
- 1 cup coconut milk
- 3 tablespoons canola oil
- 1 ½ cups vegetable broth
- 1 ½ tablespoons mild curry powder
- 3 tablespoons basil, chopped
- ½ package frozen haricots verts, cook according to instructions on the package
- Salt to taste

Method:
1. Mix together 1-tablespoon curry powder and 1-½ tablespoons oil and rub it on to the pork.
2. Place an ovenproof skillet over high heat. Add remaining oil. When oil is heated, add pork and cook until brown on all the sides.
3. Remove from heat and place the skillet in a preheated oven.
4. Bake at 350° F for about 15 minutes or until a thermometer when inserted in the center of the tenderloin shows 155° F.
5. Remove the dish from the oven and cool. When cool enough to handle, slice pork into thin slices. Transfer into a container. Cover and refrigerate until use. It can last for 4 days.
6. Pour a little coconut milk and curry powder to a saucepan and blend until smooth.
7. Add rest of the coconut milk and vegetable broth and place the saucepan over medium heat and simmer until the mixture is slightly thick.
8. Add basil and mix. Remove from heat. Transfer into a bowl. Cool and refrigerate until use
9. To serve: Heat the sauce and the slices of pork. Arrange haricots verts over individual serving plates. Place pork slices over it. Pour sauce over pork and serve.

Shepherd's Pie

Serves: 4
Cook time: 45 minutes

Ingredients:
- 1 pound ground beef
- 2 cloves garlic, minced
- 1 medium yellow onion, chopped
- 1 carrot, peeled, chopped
- 4 ounce mushrooms, sliced
- ½ bag frozen peas, thawed
- ½ can tomato paste
- 1 tablespoon balsamic vinegar
- ½ tablespoon fresh rosemary, chopped
- 1 teaspoon fresh thyme, chopped
- 2-3 medium sized sweet potatoes
- ¼ cup light coconut milk or low fat milk
- 1 ½ tablespoons butter
- Sea salt to taste
- Pepper powder to taste

Method:
1. Bake the sweet potatoes in a preheated oven at 350° F until soft. Cool.
2. When cooled, peel the sweet potatoes and mash with a potato masher. Place the mashed sweet potatoes in a bowl. Add milk, 1-tablespoon butter, sea salt and pepper. Mash well and set aside.
3. In a large skillet add ½ tablespoon butter. Keep on medium heat. Add garlic and meat. Sauté.
4. Cook until the meat is browned and keep aside.
5. To the same skillet add onions, carrots and mushrooms and sauté until the onions are pink and carrots are soft.
6. Toss the meat in the pan. Add salt, balsamic vinegar, tomato paste, rosemary and thyme.
7. Cook until the liquid is dried up.
8. Add peas. Mix well. Transfer this mixture into a large freezer safe baking dish.
9. Spread the mashed sweet potato mixture over the meat mixture.
10. Place the baking dish into a preheated oven at 350° F and bake for 15-20 minutes. Cool and refrigerate until use. It can last for 3-4 days if refrigerated or up to 2 months if frozen.

Beef and Broccoli Stir Fry

Serves: 3
Cook time: 10-12 minutes

Ingredients

- 1 pound beef, top steak, cut into ¼ inch slant slices
- 1 large head broccoli, cut into florets, slice the stalk into thin strips
- 6 cloves garlic, minced
- 2 tablespoons fresh ginger, peeled, minced
- 2 red chili peppers, minced
- 2 teaspoons crushed red pepper flakes
- 2 tablespoons apple cider vinegar
- 4 tablespoons canola oil
- 4 tablespoons tamari or coconut aminos or soy sauce
- 3 cups beef broth
- 2 tablespoons sesame seeds
- ¼ cup water

Method:

1. Mix together in a bowl, beef, soy sauce and garlic and marinate for 15-20 minutes.
2. Mix together in a small bowl, broth, vinegar, red pepper flakes and ginger root.
3. Place a large nonstick skillet over medium high heat. Add 2 tablespoons oil. When oil is heated, add only the beef and cook until brown. Remove from the pan and set aside.
4. Place the pan back on heat. Add remaining oil. When oil is heated, add broccoli and chili pepper and sauté for a minute.
5. Add water, cover and cook until broccoli is tender. Stir frequently.
6. Add broth mixture and cooked beef. Simmer for 3-4 minutes.
7. Remove from heat. Transfer into a container. Cover and refrigerate until use. It can last for 2-3 days.
8. Heat thoroughly before use. Sprinkle sesame seeds and serve.

Beef Taco Stuffed Avocadoes

Serves: 5
Cook time: 20 minutes

Ingredients:
- ½ pound ground beef
- ¼ cup onions, finely chopped
- ¼ cup bell pepper, finely chopped
- 2 green onions, thinly sliced
- 1 tablespoon olive oil
- ¼ cup sharp cheddar cheese, grated
- 5 small avocadoes, halved, pitted
- 2 teaspoons taco seasoning or more to taste
- Salt to taste

Method:
1. Place a skillet over medium heat. Add oil. When the oil is heated, add onion and bell pepper and sauté until onions are translucent.
2. Add beef and sauté until beef is nearly cooked. Add taco seasoning and salt and cook for 2-3 minutes.
3. Remove from heat and add cheese. Mix well.
4. Divide and fill the avocadoes with this mixture. Sprinkle green onions on top.
5. Place in an airtight container and refrigerate until use. It can last for 3-4 days.
6. Serve at room temperature.

Homemade Burgers

Serves: 12

Ingredients:

- 2 eggs
- 2 ½ pounds ground beef
- ½ teaspoon dried minced onion
- 2 tablespoons coconut flour
- 1 teaspoon chili powder
- 1 ½ teaspoons garlic powder
- ¼ teaspoon red pepper flakes or to taste
- 1 teaspoon dried oregano
- 1 teaspoon dried basil
- ½ teaspoon ground coriander
- Black pepper to taste
- Salt to taste
- Whole wheat burger buns to serve, as required
- Cooking spray

Method:

1. Mix together all the ingredients except burger buns in a large bowl with your hands. Shape into patties.
2. Place a nonstick pan over medium heat. Spray with cooking spray. Place patties over it and cook on both the sides.
3. Apply mayonnaise or any spread you desire.
4. Place inside the burger and serve.
5. Place the unused, uncooked burger on a baking sheet and freeze.
6. Once frozen, remove from the baking sheet and place in a freezer safe dish and freeze again.

Lamb Roast with Veggies

Serves: 2
Cook time: 2 hours

Ingredients:

- ½ pound lamb stew meat, cut into large cubes
- 2 medium tomatoes
- 1 onion, roughly chopped
- 2 cloves garlic, pressed
- 1 cup button mushrooms, halved
- 2 carrots, peeled, chopped
- 1 tablespoon fresh thyme, finely chopped
- 1 tablespoon fresh rosemary, finely chopped
- 1 cup chicken or lamb stock
- Freshly ground black pepper to taste

Method:

1. Blanch the tomatoes in boiling water until the skin just starts to crack.
2. Strain the tomatoes and place in cold water and peel the skin. Chop the tomatoes into chunks.
3. Add tomatoes to a large baking dish. Add mushrooms, carrots, onions, lamb, salt, pepper, rosemary, thyme and garlic. Mix well.
4. Place the baking dish in a preheated oven at 325° F and bake for about 2 hours or until the lamb is cooked. Stir a couple of times in between. When done, cool, cover with foil and refrigerate until use. It can last for 3-4 days.
5. Serve hot.

Zucchini Pasta Bolognese

Serves: 6
Cook time: 20 minutes

Ingredients:
- 5 whole zucchinis
- 1 can tomato paste
- 2 cans (14.5 ounces each) diced tomatoes
- 2 large yellow onions, grated
- 6 cloves garlic, crushed
- 2 pounds ground lamb
- 2 cups beef broth or chicken broth
- 1/3 cup coconut milk
- 2 cups red wine
- 2 tablespoons coconut aminos or tamari
- 2 tablespoons dried oregano
- ½ cup fresh basil leaves, chopped
- Salt to taste
- Pepper powder to taste
- 2 tablespoons olive oil or coconut oil

Method:
1. Make noodles of zucchinis by using a spiralizer or a julienne peeler and set aside.
2. Place a large saucepan over medium heat. Add oil. When oil is heated, add grated onions.
3. Sauté for a while. Add salt, pepper, and dried oregano and sauté for a couple of minutes.
4. Add garlic and sauté for a couple of minutes until fragrant. Add ground lamb and stir constantly. When beef is light brown, push the lamb all around the pan making space at the center.
5. Add tomato paste in the center and fry for a couple of minutes and slowly mix it in the beef. Add red wine and mix well. Let it cook for a while until the wine almost dries up.
6. Add tomatoes, stock and coconut aminos. Add coconut milk, stir and simmer for 5 minutes.
7. Add basil, stir and simmer for 2-3 minutes. Remove from heat and transfer into an airtight container. Refrigerate until use. It can last for 4 days.

8. To serve: Heat the Bolognese thoroughly. Place the zucchini noodles over individual serving plates. Pour sauce over the noodles and serve. If you don't like the zucchini noodles raw, then sauté in oil for 2-3 minutes.

Rosemary Lamb Chops

Serves: 6
Cook time: 10 minutes

Ingredients:
- 18 lamb chops
- 2/3 cup fresh lemon juice
- 5 cloves garlic, pressed
- Salt to taste
- Pepper to taste
- 1/3 cup fresh rosemary, chopped

Method:
1. Mix together in a bowl, all the ingredients except lamb. Rub this mixture over the lambs and set aside.
2. Place a cast iron skillet in a preheated broiler about 6-7 inches away from the heating element and heat for about 10 minutes.
3. Place the lamb chops in the skillet and broil for about 5 minutes.
4. Serve hot.
5. Store the leftover lamb chops in an airtight container in the refrigerator.
6. Heat thoroughly in an oven and serve.

Chapter 12: Side Dish Recipes

Green, Red and Yellow Rice

Serves: 4
Cook time: 8 minutes

Ingredients:
- 2 cups brown rice, rinsed, cook according to the instructions on the package
- 2 cups green onions, chopped
- ¼ cup garlic, finely chopped
- 2 cups red bell pepper, chopped
- 2 cups frozen corn, thawed
- 2 tablespoons olive oil
- 1 cup fresh cilantro, chopped
- Salt to taste
- Pepper to taste
- Cayenne pepper to taste

Method:
1. Place a large skillet over medium heat. Add oil. When the oil is heated, add garlic and sauté until fragrant. Do not burn it.
2. Add rest of the ingredients except rice and cilantro and sauté for 2-3 minutes.
3. Add rice and cilantro. Mix well and heat thoroughly. Cool and transfer into an airtight container. It can last for 2-3 days.
4. Heat thoroughly and serve.

Roasted Radishes

Serves: 4

Ingredients:
- 4 cups radishes, quartered if larger in size else halved, chop the leaves and keep aside
- 1 teaspoon sea salt or to taste
- 15 black peppercorns
- 3 sprigs fresh rosemary, chopped
- 6 tablespoon olive Oil

Method:
1. Crush together salt and peppercorns with a mortar and pestle.
2. Place together in a bowl, radishes, 4 tablespoons oil, rosemary, salt, and pepper. Toss well.
3. Transfer on to a greased baking sheet.
4. Roast in a preheated oven at 425° F until crisp and brown. Remove from oven and keep aside. Cool and refrigerate until use. It can last for 2-3 days.
5. To serve: Place a skillet over medium heat. Add the remaining oil. When the oil is heated, add the radish leaves, a little salt and sauté until wilted. Remove from heat.
6. Add the roasted radish stir well and serve immediately.

Steamed Broccoli

Serves: 6
Cook time: 4 minutes

Ingredients:
- 2 large broccoli heads, chop into florets
- 1 onion, thinly sliced
- 1 teaspoon garlic powder
- 2 teaspoons red pepper flakes
- 3 tablespoons extra virgin olive oil
- 1 teaspoon sesame oil (optional)
- Salt to taste
- Pepper to taste
- Juice of a lemon

Method:
1. Steam the broccoli for 3-4 minutes. Place the steamed broccoli in a colander. Place the colander under cold running water to stop further cooking.
2. Transfer into a large bowl. Add rest of the ingredients and toss well. Cover and refrigerate until use. It can last for 2 days.

Cucumber Bites with Feta

Serves: 4

Ingredients:

- 2 English cucumber, peeled, chopped into ¼ inch thick rounds
- Salt to taste
- Pepper to taste
- 1 cup feta
- Few small fresh basil leaves

Method:

1. Place the cucumber slices on your work area. Place about 1-2 teaspoons feta on each. Season with salt and pepper.
2. Place a basil leaf on the feta. Press slightly. Place in an airtight container. Refrigerate until use. It can last for 2-3 days.
3. Serve at room temperature.

Roasted Brussels sprouts

Serves: 3

Ingredients:
- ¾ pound Brussels sprouts, trimmed
- 1 ½ tablespoons olive oil
- Salt to taste
- Pepper to taste

Method:
1. Add all the ingredients together in a bowl. Mix well.
2. Transfer on to a baking sheet. Bake in a preheated oven at 400° F for about 30-40 minutes. Turn the Brussels sprouts a couple of times while it is roasting.
3. Transfer into an airtight container and refrigerate until use. It can last for 3-4 days.
4. Bake for a few minutes until thoroughly heated and serve.

Simply Tasty Black Beans

Serves: 5
Cook time: 2 hours

Ingredients:

- 1 cup dried black beans, soaked in water overnight, drained, rinsed
- ½ cup onions, chopped
- 1 tablespoon garlic, chopped
- ¼ cup celery, chopped
- 1 cup tomatoes, chopped
- ¼ teaspoon ground cumin
- ½ teaspoon cayenne pepper
- ½ tablespoon honey
- ¼ teaspoon ground cinnamon
- Salt to taste
- Pepper to taste
- 2 sprigs fresh thyme

Method:

1. Place a large saucepan over medium heat. Add oil. When the oil is heated, add onions, garlic and celery and sauté until onions are translucent.
2. Add tomatoes and sauté for a couple of minutes. Add cumin, cinnamon and cayenne pepper. Sauté for a few seconds until fragrant.
3. Add black beans, thyme, honey and enough water to cover the ingredients.
4. Cover and simmer until the beans are tender. If the beans are not cooked and you find there is no liquid in the saucepan, then add some hot water. The beans may take about 1-1 ½ hours to cook.
5. Add salt and pepper and cook for another 10 minutes. Discard the thyme sprigs. Transfer into a bowl. Cover and refrigerate until use. It can last for 4 days.
6. Heat thoroughly and serve.

Sweet Potato Fries

Serves: 4
Cook time: 30 minutes

Ingredients:
- 4 medium sweet potatoes, peeled, sliced into julienne strips
- 1 teaspoon chili powder
- 1 teaspoon pepper powder
- 1 teaspoon cumin powder
- ½ teaspoon cayenne pepper
- Sea salt to taste
- 2 tablespoons extra virgin olive oil

Method:
1. Add all the ingredients into a bowl and toss well.
2. Transfer on to a greased baking sheet and spread it in a single layer. Bake in batches if necessary
3. Bake in a preheated oven 425° F for about 30 minutes or until light brown in color. It should be tender. Turn the sweet potatoes half way through baking. Transfer into an airtight container. Refrigerate until use. It can last for 4-5 days.
4. To serve: Bake in a preheated oven for a few minutes until crisp on the outside.

Potato Rounds with Fresh Lemon

Serves: 6
Cook time: 20 minutes

Ingredients:

- 1 ½ pounds fingerling potatoes, scrubbed, sliced into 1/8 inch thick rounds
- 3 teaspoons dried oregano
- 1 ½ tablespoons extra virgin olive oil, divided
- 3 teaspoons lemon zest, grated
- Coarsely ground black pepper to taste
- Salt to taste

Method:

1. Add potatoes, pepper, oregano and half the oil into a bowl and toss well.
2. Transfer on to a greased baking sheet and spread it in a single layer. Bake in batches if necessary.
3. Bake in a preheated oven 450° F for about 20 minutes or until golden brown in color. It should be tender inside and crisp outside. Turn the potatoes half way through baking.
5. When done, remove from the oven. Transfer into an airtight container. Refrigerate until use. It can last for 4-5 days.
6. To serve: Bake in a preheated oven for a few minutes until crisp on the outside.
4. Sprinkle remaining oil, lemon zest and salt and toss well. Serve immediately.

Cauliflower Rice

Ingredients:

- 2 heads cauliflower, chopped into florets
- 1 onion, finely diced
- 4 tablespoons olive oil
- 4 cloves garlic, minced
- Salt to taste
- Pepper powder to taste

Method:

1. Add the cauliflower florets into the food processor and pulse until you get a rice like texture. You can also grate the cauliflower.
2. Place a large skillet over medium high heat. Add oil. When oil is heated, add onions and sauté until translucent. Add garlic and sauté until fragrant.
3. Add cauliflower rice and sauté for about 5-6 minutes. Transfer into an airtight container and refrigerate until use. It can last for 3-4 days.
4. To serve: Heat thoroughly. Sprinkle salt and pepper just before serving.

Butternut Squash Sauté

Ingredients:

- 2 small butternut squash, peeled, deseeded, chopped into ½ inch cubes
- 2 teaspoons ground cumin
- 2 tablespoons olive oil
- 1 teaspoon ground cinnamon
- Freshly ground black pepper to taste
- Salt to taste

Method:

1. Place a skillet over high heat. Add oil. When the oil is heated, add squash and toss well.
2. Add rest of the ingredients and sauté until tender and brown on the outside. Toss frequently. Store in an airtight container in the refrigerator until use. It can last for 2-3 days.
3. Heat thoroughly and immediately.

Stir-fry Cabbage

Ingredients:
- 1 medium head cabbage, shredded
- 2 teaspoons sesame oil
- 2 teaspoons Chinese five spice powder
- 2 teaspoons liquid aminos or soy sauce
- 2 tablespoons sesame seeds

Method:
1. Place a skillet over high heat. Add oil. When the oil is heated, add cabbage and sauté.
2. Add rest of the ingredients and sauté until tender. Toss frequently. Store in an airtight container in the refrigerator until use. It can last for 2-3 days.
3. Heat thoroughly and serve hot.

Roasted Mushrooms with Thyme

Serves: 4-6
Cook time: 25 minutes

Ingredients:
- 2 pounds cremini mushrooms
- 15 fresh thyme sprigs
- 4 tablespoons olive oil
- 8 cloves garlic, minced
- 1 tablespoon ghee or coconut oil
- Sea salt to taste
- Freshly ground black pepper to taste

Method:
1. Place an ovenproof skillet over medium heat. Add ghee. When the ghee melts, add garlic and thyme. Sauté for a few seconds until fragrant. Remove from heat.
2. Place the mushrooms in the skillet over the garlic and thyme with the cap side down. Sprinkle salt and pepper.
3. Sprinkle olive oil all over the mushrooms.
4. Bake in a preheated oven at 375° F for about 20-25 minutes.
5. Remove the skillet from the oven. Cool and place the skillet in the refrigerator until use. It can last for 2-3 days.
6. To serve: Place the skillet in the oven and heat thoroughly. Mix well with the drippings in the skillet and serve.

Southwestern Cheddar Steak Fries

Serves: 6
Cook time: 19 minutes

Ingredients:

- 1 ½ pounds red or Yukon gold potatoes, scrubbed, cut lengthwise into ¾ inch wedges
- ½ cup red bell pepper, finely chopped
- 3 teaspoons smoked paprika
- 1 teaspoon garlic powder
- 1 teaspoon ground cumin
- 1.5 ounces reduced fat sharp cheddar cheese, finely shredded
- 3 tablespoons fresh cilantro, finely chopped
- 4 teaspoons extra virgin olive oil
- Salt to taste

Method:

1. Add potatoes, paprika, garlic powder, cumin and oil into a bowl and toss well.
2. Transfer on to a greased baking sheet and spread it in a single layer. Bake in batches if necessary.
3. Bake in a preheated oven 425° F for about 20 minutes or until golden brown in color. It should be tender inside and crisp outside. Turn the potatoes half way through baking.
4. When done, remove from the oven. Cool and transfer into an airtight container.
5. To serve: Place potatoes on a baking sheet. Sprinkle salt, pepper and cheese.
6. Place the baking sheet in the oven. Bake for a few minutes until the cheese melts.
7. Garnish with cilantro and serve immediately.

Chapter 13: Dessert Recipes

Chocolate Pudding

Serves: 8

Ingredients:
- 1 cup almond milk
- 4 ripe avocados, peeled, pitted, chopped
- ½ cup honey or to taste
- 2 teaspoons vanilla extract
- 2/3 cup cocoa powder, or more if you like a stronger taste, unsweetened

Method:
1. Blend together all the ingredients in a blender smooth.
2. Pour into individual dessert bowls. Chill until use and serve. It can last for 3-4 days.

Black Forest Banana Split

Serves: 4

Ingredients:
- 4 bananas, peeled, halved lengthwise
- 4 cups non fat ricotta cheese
- 32 walnut halves
- 4 teaspoons cherry concentrate
- 2 teaspoons cocoa powder, unsweetened

Method:
1. Place a cup of ricotta cheese on 4 serving plates. Place a halved banana on either side of the cheese.
2. Sprinkle cocoa all over. Top with walnuts. Drizzle a teaspoon of cherry concentrate over it.
3. Chill until use. It can last for 2 days.

Coconut and Chia seed Pudding

Serves: 6

Ingredients:

- ½ cup shredded, unsweetened coconut
- ½ cup chia seeds
- 1 ½ cups full fat coconut milk
- 1 cup coconut water
- 2 teaspoons pure vanilla extract
- ½ teaspoon salt
- 1 cup fresh raspberries to serve

Method:

1. Mix together all the ingredients except raspberries in a bowl.
2. Pour into serving bowls and refrigerate until use.
3. Serve with fresh raspberries.

Puffed Quinoa Peanut Butter Balls

Serves: 12-15
Cook time: 5-8 minutes

Ingredients:
- 2 cups puffed quinoa
- 1 cup peanut butter
- ½ cup agave nectar or honey or pure maple syrup
- 2 tablespoons peanuts, roasted, crushed
- 2 teaspoons vanilla extract
- Dark chocolate, melted for dipping (optional)

Method:
1. Mix together in a heatproof bowl, peanut butter, agave and vanilla. Place the bowl in a double boiler until the ingredients are softened and smooth flowing. Whisk as it is softening.
2. Remove from heat and add puffed quinoa. Mix well and refrigerate for 15-20 minutes.
3. Remove from the refrigerator and divide the mixture into 12-15 equal portions and shape into small balls. Dip into dark chocolate if desired. Refrigerate until set. It can store for a week.

No Bake Cookies

Serves: 20-25

Ingredients:
- ½ cup natural almond butter or any other nut butter of your choice
- 8 scoops vanilla or chocolate protein powder
- 2 tablespoons ground flaxseeds
- 4 cups rolled oats
- 2 teaspoons cocoa powder, unsweetened
- 1 cup water
- ¼ cup raisins
- 2 tablespoons dried cranberries
- 2 tablespoons walnuts, chopped

Method:
1. Mix together all the ingredients in a bowl to form dough like consistency.
2. Shape into cookies and place on a dish which is lined with parchment paper.
3. Refrigerate until use. It can last for a week.

Strawberry/ Blueberry Ice cream

Serves: 10

Ingredients:
- 2 cups coconut milk
- ½ pound frozen strawberries /blueberries, unsweetened
- Stevia or sugar to taste
- ¼ tablespoon lemon juice or to taste

Method:
1. Place all ingredients in the food processor and blend until smooth.
2. Transfer into a freezer safe container.
3. Freeze until firm.
4. Alternately transfer the blended mixture into an ice cream maker and follow the manufacturer's instructions to freeze.
5. Remove from the freezer 30 minutes before serving.
6. Scoop and serve in dessert bowls.

Orange Berry Parfait

Serve: 2

Ingredients:

- ½ cups orange juice
- ¼ cup chia seeds
- 2 tablespoons agave nectar or maple syrup or sweetener of your choice
- 1 banana, sliced
- 1 cup fresh berries of your choice

Method:

1. Pour orange juice in a bowl. Add chia seeds. Stir well. Cover and keep it aside for 10 minutes. Stir in between. If all the orange juice has not been absorbed by the chia seeds, then blend with a stick blender.
2. Divide the chia seeds into 2 glasses. Layer alternately with berries and bananas.
3. Chill and serve later. It can store for 2 days.

Strawberry Mousse

Serves: 6

Ingredients:

- 3 cups strawberries, sliced
- 3 cups firm tofu, drained, crumbled
- Sweetener of your choice (agave nectar or honey or stevia drops)
- A few strawberries, sliced to serve

Method:

1. Add strawberries into a blender. Blend the strawberries. Add tofu and sweetener and blend until smooth.
2. Transfer into individual serving bowls and refrigerate for a few hours before serving.
3. Garnish with sliced strawberries and serve. It can store for 3-4 days.

Pumpkin Pie Yogurt Parfait

Serves: 4

Ingredients:

- 12 ounces coconut milk yogurt
- ½ cup pumpkin puree
- 1 teaspoon pumpkin pie spice
- 2 tablespoons pumpkin seeds (pepitas)
- A little honey

Method:

1. Mix together pumpkin puree, pumpkin pie spice and yogurt to a bowl and mix well.
2. Transfer into individual dessert bowls. Garnish with pumpkin seeds. Drizzle a bit of honey over it.
3. Chill and serve later. It can store for 2-3 days.

Nutty Blueberry Protein Balls

Serves: 15-18

Ingredients:
- 8 prunes, pitted
- 1 cup fresh strawberries, chopped
- 1 cup macadamia nuts, unsalted, roasted
- 2 cups walnuts or almonds
- 1 cup shredded coconut, unsweetened
- 4 tablespoons coconut oil, melted

Method:
1. Place the prunes in the food processor bowl and pulse until smooth.
2. Add walnuts or almonds and macadamia nuts. Pulse until the nuts are finely chopped.
3. With the food processor running, slowly pour melted coconut oil. Keep the food processor running until the oil is being poured.
4. Transfer the mixture into a bowl. Add strawberries and mix well to form dough. Shape the dough into small balls of any size you desire.
5. Place the shredded coconut on a plate. Roll the balls in the shredded coconut and place on another plate.
6. Refrigerate the balls until ready to serve.
7. Keep the unused ones refrigerated. It can last for 4-5 days when refrigerated.

Carrot Cake Energy Bites

Serves: 20

Ingredients:

- ½ cup walnuts
- 12 medjool dates, pitted
- ½ cup finely shredded coconut + extra to top
- 1 cup carrots, finely grated + extra to top
- ¼ teaspoon sea salt
- 1 teaspoon ground nutmeg

Method:

1. Add dates, ½ cup carrots, coconut, salt and nutmeg into a food processor and pulse until smooth.
2. Add remaining carrots and walnuts and pulse until you get a coarse texture with the nuts visible.
3. Transfer into a bowl. Divide and shape into 20 balls. Roll each in extra shredded coconut and place on a lined baking sheet. Garnish with carrots and serve.
4. Refrigerate the balls until ready to serve.
5. Keep the unused ones refrigerated. It can last for 4-5 days when refrigerated.

Honey-Broiled Nectarines

Serves: 4
Cook time: 6-8 minutes

Ingredients:
- 2 large nectarines, pitted, halved
- 1 tablespoon lemon juice
- 3 tablespoons honey

Method:
1. Place the nectarine halves with its cut side facing up in a baking dish.
2. Mix together honey and lemon juice in a bowl.
3. Brush this mixture over the nectarines.
4. Broil in a preheated broiler for 6-8 minutes.
5. Serve warm.
6. To store, place in an airtight container and refrigerate until use.
7. Heat in a preheated oven for 2-3 minutes and serve